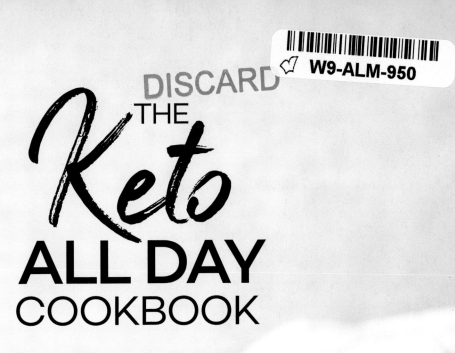

THE
Keto
ALL DAY
COOKBOOK

MORE THAN 100 LOW-CARB RECIPES THAT LET YOU STAY KETO
FOR BREAKFAST, LUNCH, AND DINNER

MARTINA SLAJEROVA

FAIR WINDS

Brimming with creative inspiration, how-to projects, and useful information to enrich your everyday life, Quarto Knows is a favorite destination for those pursuing their interests and passions. Visit our site and dig deeper with our books into your area of interest: Quarto Creates, Quarto Cooks, Quarto Homes, Quarto Lives, Quarto Drives, Quarto Explores, Quarto Gifts, or Quarto Kids.

First Published in 2019 by Fair Winds Press, an imprint of The Quarto Group,
100 Cummings Center, Suite 265-D, Beverly, MA 01915, USA.
T (978) 282-9590 F (978) 283-2742 QuartoKnows.com

Fair Winds Press titles are also available at discount for retail, wholesale, promotional, and bulk purchase. For details, contact the Special Sales Manager by email at specialsales@quarto.com or by mail at The Quarto Group, Attn: Special Sales Manager, 100 Cummings Center, Suite 265-D, Beverly, MA 01915.

23 22 21 20 19   4 5 6 7 8

ISBN: 978-1-59233-870-2

Digital edition published in 2019
eISBN: 978-1-63159-678-0

Library of Congress Cataloging-in-Publication Data is available

Design and Page Layout: Rita Sowins / Sowins Design
Cover Images: Martina Slajerova
Photography: Martina Slajerova

Printed in Canada

Some of the recipes in *The Keto All Day Cookbook* previously appeared in the following books by Martina Slajerova: *The KetoDiet Cookbook, Sweet & Savory Fat Bombs, Quick Keto Meals in 30 Minutes or Less, Keto Slow Cooker & One-Pot Meals*, and *The Beginner's KetoDiet Cookbook*.

The information in this book is for educational purposes only. It is not intended to replace the advice of a physician or medical practitioner. Please see your health-care provider before beginning any new health program.

Contents

INTRODUCTION	4
HOW TO USE THIS BOOK	6
1. KETO-FRIENDLY HOMEMADE BASICS	8
2. SATIATING, FAT-FUELED BREAKFASTS	18
3. SATISFYING KETO SNACKS AND APPETIZERS	44
4. STICK-TO-YOUR-RIBS SOUPS AND HEARTY SALADS	54
5. EASY, LOW-STARCH LUNCHES	74
6. HIGH-FAT DINNERS ALL WEEK LONG	90
7. SUGAR-FREE DRINKS AND DESSERTS	138
8. EXTRAS: SAUCES, MARINADES, AND MUCH MORE	158
ABOUT THE AUTHOR	172
ACKNOWLEDGMENTS	172
INDEX	173

Introduction

Before I discovered low-carb eating, I followed what most people considered to be a healthy lifestyle. The general advice was to eat less, avoid dietary fats, and exercise more. So I did just that. But instead of improving my health, I developed thyroid issues and started gaining weight. And all this happened because I was following what I believed to be the "right" approach.

I couldn't understand what I was doing wrong until I learned that the general dietary recommendations are based on bad science. For decades we've been avoiding saturated fat and cholesterol for fear of increasing our risk of heart disease. We've been told that eating five small meals a day is better for you than eating three regular meals. We've been told that most of our daily energy intake should come from carbohydrates. So we replaced saturated fats with carbohydrates, and we've started eating breakfast cereals instead of eggs. We are now living in a world where carbohydrate and sugar consumption have reached new heights. That, in turn, has led to an obesity epidemic, plus an increase in diagnoses of type 2 diabetes, cardiovascular disease, lipid problems, inflammation, and hypertension.

The truth is simple: Healthy eating doesn't have to be complicated, and you don't need to starve to lose weight. When you eat real food that's low in carbs, moderate in protein, and high in fat, you will achieve weight loss by balancing the hormones that control appetite and fat utilization (insulin, ghrelin, and leptin). You simply need to adopt a healthy lifestyle that's also sustainable, so that you'll never feel like "dieting" and depriving yourself of tasty foods.

That's why the ketogenic diet works so well for me. It's not just a diet, it's a lifestyle. Unlike other dietary approaches, once you learn the basic principles, it's easy to follow and it's easy to stick with in the long term. You will enjoy the food because fat tastes good and will keep you fuller for longer.

I've written five cookbooks with recipes suitable for a keto diet, and this book features some of my all-time favorites, plus dishes that have gotten rave reviews from my friends, family, and—most importantly—my readers. It's not always easy to stay on track when you're following a ketogenic lifestyle, especially when you're new to it or when life gets busy and stressful. That's why it's so important that the recipes in this book are easy to make and irresistibly delicious. Assembling them has been so much fun: as a passionate cook, I love nothing more than experimenting with ingredients and flavor combinations and giving tried-and-true recipes a fresh twist. The Raspberry Electrolyte Limeade (page 155) is a great example: it's a new, more flavorful take on my basic version of the recipe, which has gone viral over social media. Sometimes an accidental dessert, such as the Cookie Dough Mousse (page 147), turns out to be a huge success and you end up making it over and over (and over!) again.

If you love the convenience of one-pot meals but don't want to compromise on taste, try the Thai Curry Chicken Tray Bake (page 102) or Harissa Fish Tray Bake (page 100). For more family favorites, check out some of my slow-cooker classics, such as Moussaka (page 136) and Beef Short Ribs with coleslaw (page 130). They're serious crowd-pleasers, but they call for only minimum prep time.

Some recipes, like my Keto Cheese Sauce (page 12), Keto Tortillas (page 11), and Pizza (page 124) are so good that I created several variations of each of them. (I just couldn't stop!) And I always make a few batches of Flavored Butter (page 14), freeze it, and then use it to top veggies or steak to give them an instant boost of flavor and healthy fats. Speaking of healthy fats, if there's a single ingredient I can't live without, it's avocado. It's not just high in electrolytes and healthy fats; it's also incredibly versatile. Stuff avocadoes with chicken, fish, or vegetables for an instant lunch (page 73), and use them in smoothies or as an ingredient in Key Lime Pie in a Jar (page 145).

This book also includes keto-friendly recipes from around the world. Look for American classics like Speedy Cauliflower-n-Cheese (page 117), a Healthy Deconstructed Hamburger (page 127); and sugar-free Boston Cream Pie (page 150). I've also added some Asian favorites, like Keto Kung Pao Chicken (page 114) and Butter Chicken (page 106), and continental dishes like Hungarian Goulash (page 66), and Coq au Vin (page 105). Many of my readers know that I was born in the Czech Republic, and some of the dishes here are based on family recipes, like the Czech Butter Cake (page 144) and Creamy "Potato" Soup (page 65). Others were inspired by my partner Nikos's Greek origins and his own family recipes: the Greek Meatball Soup (page 60) is beyond delicious, and the Cheese-Stuffed Greek Bifteki (page 137) is based on a type of Greek street food that we discovered on our holiday travels.

There are plenty of brand-new recipes here, too. Dig into my chocolaty, low-carb "No-Tella" Granola (page 40) for breakfast; pack a couple Ham & Cheese Bread Rolls (page 86) in your backpack or briefcase for a low-starch lunch; and treat yourself and your family to the Bacon-Wrapped Chorizo Meatloaf (page 128) for a satisfying keto dinner.

I hope the recipes in this book will make following a keto lifestyle fun and easy. Enjoy!

How to Use This Book

USE WHOLE FOODS

When you're sourcing ingredients, go for organic and additive-free. Buy organic eggs, organic unwaxed lemons, pastured beef and butter, outdoor-reared pork, wild-caught fish, and extra-virgin olive oil.

REMEMBER

Nutrition values for each recipe in this book are per serving unless stated otherwise. The nutrition data are derived from the USDA National Nutrient Database (ndb.nal.usda.gov).

Nutrition facts are calculated from edible parts. For example, if one large avocado is listed as 200 g/7.1 oz, this value represents its edible parts (pit and peel removed) unless otherwise specified.

Optional ingredients and suggested sides and toppings are not included in the nutrition information. You can use raw cacao powder and unsweetened cocoa powder (Dutch process) interchangeably.

Ingredients such as cream cheese, ricotta, or Halloumi cheese are all full-fat unless otherwise specified.

All ingredients should be sugar-free, unless you use dark 85% to 90% chocolate, which contains a small and acceptable amount of sugar.

ICONS

All recipes are tagged with the following icons, as needed:

dairy-free

vegetarian

nut-free

ideal for intermittent fasting

egg-free

high in electrolytes

nightshade-free

induction-friendly

The "induction-friendly" icon indicates which recipes are most suitable for the initial phase of the ketogenic diet. Certain foods such as low-carb treats, bread, or even roasted nuts may cause cravings and stall your progress.

The "ideal for intermittent fasting" icon indicates recipes with higher protein and fat content, and are thus ideal for those who skip meals. Apart from high-protein and high-calorie recipes, sweet and savory fat bombs are also suitable for intermittent fasting. Finally, my Raspberry Electrolyte Limeade (page 155) and Bone Broth (page 160) will help you stay hydrated and at the same time get the optimal level of magnesium, potassium, and sodium.

The "high in electrolytes" icon indicates which recipes are high in electrolytes, especially magnesium and potassium. Sufficient intake of electrolytes is vital during the induction phase of the ketogenic diet and for minimizing any side effects of carbohydrate withdrawal also known as "keto flu."

OPTIONAL INGREDIENTS

Optional ingredients, suggested sides, and suggested alternatives and toppings are not included in the nutrition information. If allergy-free options are included, such recipes are tagged with the same icons as shown at the left, only in gray:　　,　　etc.

CAULIFLOWER RICE
THREE WAYS, PAGE 13

CHAPTER 1

KETO-FRIENDLY HOMEMADE
Basics

ABOVE: SOURDOUGH KETO BUNS, PAGE 10
FLAVORED BUTTER TWELVE WAYS, PAGE 14

KETO TORTILLAS THREE WAYS, PAGE 11

KETO CHEESE SAUCE THREE WAYS, PAGE 12

FOLLOWING A LOW-CARB LIFESTYLE IS SO MUCH EASIER (AND TASTIER!) when you have a handful of basic keto staples in your repertoire. Sure, it might be tempting to take shortcuts and go for store-bought stuff, but sugar, additives, and other unhealthy ingredients often lurk in mass-produced products, so you're better off making homemade versions of things you're going to use frequently in your keto kitchen.

That's where this chapter comes in. Here, you'll learn how easy it is to make the go-to ingredients you'll reach for just about every day. If you miss bread the most, try the Sourdough Keto Buns on page 10; they're incredibly fluffy, and are perfect as sides or as the base for low-carb sandwiches. Same goes for the Keto Tortillas Three Ways on page 11, which, if you ask me, taste even better than the real thing. And with the Flavored Butter Twelve Ways on page 14, you'll be able to add extra flavor (and good-for-you fats) to any sweet or savory meal.

All this makes sticking to clean, low-carb eating simpler—and that'll help you reach your long-term goals. Let's get started!

HOMEMADE DARK CHOCOLATE THREE WAYS, PAGE 16

Sourdough Keto Buns

8 REGULAR OR 16 MINI BUNS
HANDS-ON TIME: 15 MINUTES
OVERALL TIME: 1 HOUR

DRY INGREDIENTS

1½ cups (150 g/5.3 oz) almond flour

⅓ cup (40 g/1.4 oz) psyllium husk powder

½ cup (60 g/2.1 oz) coconut flour

½ cup (75 g/2.7 oz) firmly packed flax meal

1 teaspoon baking soda

1 teaspoon fine sea salt

WET INGREDIENTS

6 large egg whites

2 large eggs

¾ cup (180 ml) low-fat buttermilk (see tips)

¼ cup (60 ml) apple cider vinegar

1 cup (240 ml) lukewarm water

I absolutely adore this bread recipe, and I think it even beats the regular, high-carb version! These buns are incredibly fluffy, and they remind me of the loaves of rustic bread my grandmother used to make. And they're a great accompaniment to just about anything, so be sure to keep a batch on hand in the freezer.

Preheat the oven to 350°F (180°C, or gas mark 4). Mix all the dry ingredients in a bowl. In a separate bowl, mix the egg whites, eggs, and buttermilk. Add the egg mixture to the dry mixture, and process well using a mixer until the dough is thick. Add the vinegar and lukewarm water, and process until well combined. Do not overprocess the dough. Using a spoon, make 8 regular or 16 mini buns. Place them on a baking tray lined with parchment paper or a nonstick mat, leaving some space between them.

Transfer them to the oven and bake for 10 minutes. Reduce the temperature to 300°F (150°C, or gas mark 2) and bake for another 30 to 45 minutes (small buns will take less time to cook). Remove from the oven, let them cool, and place the buns on a rack to cool to room temperature. Store them at room temperature if you plan to use them in the next couple of days or store in the freezer for up to 3 months.

NOTES:

- For best results, use a kitchen scale to weigh all the dry ingredients.
- Do not use full-fat buttermilk or the buns will end up too dense.
- I've always had best results when using whole psyllium husks that I powder myself in a coffee grinder. Store-bought psyllium husk powder will work, too, but the buns may be denser. Baked goods that use psyllium always result in a slightly moist texture. If needed, cut the buns in half and place in a toaster or in the oven before serving.
- To save time, mix all the dry ingredients ahead and store in a resealable bag and add a label with the number of servings. When ready to be baked, just add the wet ingredients!

NUTRITION FACTS PER MINI BUN: Total carbs: 7 g | Fiber: 4.8 g | Net carbs: 2.2 g | Protein: 6.1 g | Fat: 8.2 g | Calories: 116 kcal
MACRONUTRIENT RATIO: Calories from carbs (8%), protein (23%), fat (69%)

Keto Tortillas Three Ways

10 TORTILLAS
HANDS-ON TIME: 20 MINUTES
OVERALL TIME: 20 MINUTES + CHILLING

BASIC INGREDIENTS

1 cup (100 g/3.5 oz) almond flour

½ cup (75 g/2.7 oz) firmly packed flax meal

¼ cup (30 g/1.1 oz) coconut flour

2 tablespoons (8 g/0.3 oz) whole psyllium husks

2 tablespoons (15 g/0.5 oz) ground chia seeds

1 teaspoon fine sea salt

2 tablespoons (30 g/1.1 oz) ghee or virgin coconut oil

FOR SPINACH TORTILLAS

2 cups (312 g/11 oz) frozen spinach, thawed, drained, and puréed

1 teaspoon ground cumin

¾ cup (180 ml) lukewarm water, plus a few tablespoons if the dough is too dry

FOR PESTO TORTILLAS

3 tablespoons (45 g/1.6 oz) Red Pesto (page 168)

½ cup (45 g/1.6 oz) grated Parmesan

1 cup (240 ml) lukewarm water, plus a few tablespoons if the dough is too dry

FOR CURRIED TORTILLAS

2 tablespoons (30 g/1.1 oz) curry paste

1 cup (240 ml) lukewarm water, plus a few tablespoons if the dough is too dry

Note: It works with harissa paste, too!

These tortillas take their inspiration from one of the most popular recipes on my blog. Their taste and texture is just like their high-carb counterparts: they're soft, tender, and easy to roll and fold. Stuff them with just about anything—from veggies and avocado slices to egg salad to grilled salmon—or slather them with guacamole for a snack.

Combine all the basic ingredients, apart from the cooking fat. Add all the other ingredients needed to make spinach, pesto, or curried tortillas. (If making spinach tortillas, drain the frozen spinach and discard the excess water. Place in a blender and process until puréed.) If the dough is too dry to roll, add a few more tablespoons of water. Mix well using your hands and shape into an oval. Let the dough rest in the fridge for up to 1 hour.

When ready, remove the dough from the fridge and cut it into 6 equal pieces. (You will make the remaining 4 tortillas using the excess dough.) Place a piece of the dough between 2 pieces of parchment paper and roll it out until very thin. Alternatively, use a silicone roller and a silicone mat.

Remove the top parchment paper. Press a large 8-inch (20-cm) lid into the dough (or use a piece of parchment paper to cut into a round shape). Trace around it with your knife to cut out the tortilla.

Repeat for the remaining pieces of dough. Add the cut-off excess dough to the last piece and create the remaining 4 tortillas from it. If you have any dough left over, simply roll it out and cut it into tortilla-chip shapes.

Grease a large pan with ghee and cook 1 tortilla at a time over medium heat for 2 to 3 minutes on each side until lightly browned. Don't overcook it. Once cool, store the tortillas in an airtight container for up to 1 week and reheat them in a dry pan, if needed.

NUTRITION FACTS PER TORTILLA (SPINACH/PESTO/CURRIED): Total carbs: 8.7/7.9/7.8 g | Fiber: 6.7/5.9/5.8 g | Net carbs: 2/2/2 g | Protein: 6.2/6.8/5.1 g | Fat: 14.2/17/14 g | Calories: 176/202/168 kcal
MACRONUTRIENT RATIO: Calories from carbs (5/4/5%), protein (15/15/13%), fat (80/81/82%)

Keto Cheese Sauce Three Ways

4 SERVINGS (ABOUT 1 CUP/240 ML)
HANDS-ON TIME: 5 MINUTES
OVERALL TIME: 5 MINUTES

BASIC INGREDIENTS

¼ cup (60 ml) heavy whipping cream
2 tablespoon (28 g/1 oz) unsalted
   butter or ghee
¼ cup (60 g/2.1 oz) cream cheese
Optional: Salt and pepper

1 to 2 tablespoons (15 to 30 ml)
   water or cream, for thinning sauce

FOR SRIRACHA CHEESE SAUCE

½ cup (57 g/2 oz) grated Cheddar
1 tablespoon (15 ml) Sriracha sauce

FOR MEDITERRANEAN CHEESE SAUCE

½ cup (45 g/1.6 oz) grated Parmesan
   or goat cheese
½ teaspoon onion powder
¼ teaspoon garlic powder
1 tablespoon (5 g/0.2 oz) chopped
   fresh basil, or 1 teaspoon dried
   basil
1 teaspoon fresh lemon zest

FOR BLUE CHEESE SAUCE

½ cup (68 g/2.4 oz) crumbled blue
   cheese

This Keto Cheese Sauce is based on one of my most popular blog recipes: It calls for a handful of basic ingredients, takes just a few minutes to whip up, and you can serve it with pretty much anything, from roasted chicken to pan-seared salmon to steamed veggies. (I'm not supposed to play favorites, but I have to confess that I'm pretty partial to the blue cheese variation!)

Pour the cream into a small saucepan, and add the butter and cream cheese. Gently bring to a simmer over medium-low heat, and stir until well combined and the cream cheese and butter are melted. Once simmering, cook for about a minute while stirring. Then remove from the heat. If you need to thicken the sauce, continue to simmer for 3 to 5 more minutes, stirring frequently. Season with salt and pepper, if desired.

TO MAKE THE SRIRACHA CHEESE SAUCE: Add the Cheddar. Stir until the Cheddar is completely melted and the sauce is smooth and creamy. Then add the Sriracha, and stir again until combined.

TO MAKE THE MEDITERRANEAN CHEESE SAUCE: Add the Parmesan. Stir until the cheese is completely melted and the sauce is smooth and creamy. Then add the remaining ingredients, and stir again until combined.

TO MAKE THE BLUE CHEESE SAUCE: Add the blue cheese. Stir until the cheese is completely melted and the sauce is smooth and creamy.

The cheese sauce is best served immediately. Reheating may cause splitting. If you do need to reheat the sauce and it splits, add a splash of hot water and stir well, or, if that doesn't work, blitz it in a blender to recombine.

NOTE:
If the sauce is too thick, add a splash of water or cream to thin it down.

NUTRITION FACTS PER SERVING (¼ CUP/60 ML SRIRACHA/MEDITERRANEAN/BLUE CHEESE SAUCE): Total carbs: 1.8/1.8/1.3 g | Fiber: 0.1/0.2/0 g | Net carbs: 1.7/1.6/1.3 g | Protein: 4.7/5.5/5 g | Fat: 20.6/18.6/20.5 g | Calories: 203/189/202 kcal
MACRONUTRIENT RATIO: Calories from carbs (3/3/2%), protein (9/11/10%), fat (88/86/88%)

Cauliflower Rice Three Ways

4 SERVINGS
HANDS-ON TIME: 15 MINUTES
OVERALL TIME: 15 MINUTES

BASIC INGREDIENTS

1 medium (720 g/1.6 lb) cauliflower
2 tablespoons (30 g/1.1 oz) ghee or
    virgin coconut oil
Salt and freshly ground black pepper

MASALA CAULI-RICE

1 teaspoon garam masala
½ teaspoon onion powder
¼ teaspoon turmeric powder
⅛ teaspoon chili powder

LEMON & HERB CAULI-RICE

2 tablespoons (8 g/0.3 oz) fresh
    herbs, such as basil, oregano,
    thyme, and parsley
1 teaspoon fresh lemon zest
½ teaspoon garlic powder

SPANISH CAULI-RICE

½ teaspoon onion powder
½ teaspoon garlic powder
2 tablespoons (30 g/1.1 oz)
    unsweetened tomato paste

Who needs starchy side dishes when (fiber- and vitamin-C-packed) cauliflower rice is so easy to make? It's a keto kitchen staple because it literally goes with just about everything: Pair it with roasted meat, top it with low-carb chili, or use it to soak up flavorful sauces.

Run the cauliflower florets through a hand grater or food processor with a grating blade. Pulse until the florets resemble grains of rice.

Grease a large saucepan with ghee and add all the aromatics for the preferred cauli-rice recipe: Masala, Lemon & Herb, or Spanish. Mix and cook over medium-low heat for up to 1 minute. Add the cauliflower rice and cook for 5 to 7 minutes, stirring constantly. Season with salt and pepper, and serve with slow-cooked meat and sauce. To store, let it cool and place in an airtight container. Refrigerate for up to 5 days.

NUTRITION FACTS PER SERVING (ABOUT 1 CUP/125 G MASALA/LEMON & HERB/SPANISH CAULI-RICE): Total carbs: 9.6/9.4/10.2 g | Fiber: 3.8/3.7/3.9 g | Net carbs: 5.8/5.7/6.3 g | Protein: 3.6/3.6/3.7 g | Fat: 8.1/8/8 g | Calories: 116/115/118 kcal
MACRONUTRIENT RATIO: Calories from carbs (21/21/3%), protein (13/13/13%), fat (66/66/64%)

Flavored Butter Twelve Ways

EACH RECIPE: 4 TO 6 OUNCES
(113 TO 168 G) FLAVORED BUTTER
HANDS-ON TIME: 10 MINUTES
OVERALL TIME: 30 MINUTES

SAVORY BUTTERS

½ cup (113 g/4 oz) softened
  unsalted butter
¼ to ½ teaspoon sea salt (or less,
  if other salty ingredients are
  added)
¼ teaspoon black pepper

Having a repertoire of flavored butters on hand makes life so much easier when you're short on time. That way, you'll never have to skimp on taste—even when you've only got minutes to whip up a meal. And, of course, they're all a rich source of healthy fats. Feel free to substitute ghee, lard, duck fat, or even virgin coconut oil in any of the versions below.

GARLIC & HERB BUTTER

2 tablespoons (30 ml) extra-virgin
  olive oil
4 cloves garlic, crushed
2 tablespoons (8 g/0.3 oz) chopped
  parsley or 2 teaspoons dried
  parsley

BACON & CHEESE BUTTER

2 large slices (32 g/1.1 oz) crisp
  bacon, crumbled
½ cup (28 g/1 oz) grated Cheddar
  cheese
1 to 2 tablespoons (4 to 8 g/0.2 to
  0.3 oz) chopped chives or spring
  onion

JALAPEÑO & LIME BUTTER

1 medium (14 g/0.5 oz) jalapeño
  pepper, deseeded and finely
  chopped
1 tablespoon (15 ml) fresh lime juice
1 to 2 tablespoons (4 to 8 g/0.2 to
  0.3 oz) chopped cilantro

SPICY HARISSA BUTTER

3 tablespoons (45 g/1.6 oz) harissa
  paste

THAI CURRY BUTTER

2 tablespoons (30 g/1.1 oz) Thai
  curry paste

LEMON & HERB BUTTER

1 tablespoon (15 ml) fresh lemon
  juice
2 teaspoons (4 g/0.1 oz) fresh
  lemon zest
2 cloves garlic, crushed
1 to 2 tablespoons (4 to 8 g/
  0.2 to 0.3 oz) chopped herbs,
  such as basil, dill, or thyme, or
  1 to 2 teaspoons (2 g/0.1 oz) dried
  herbs

WALNUT & BLUE CHEESE BUTTER

⅓ cup (45 g/1.6 oz) crumbled blue
  cheese
¼ cup (25 g/0.9 oz) chopped
  walnuts or pecans
1 teaspoon onion powder
1 to 2 tablespoons (4 to 8 g/0.2 to
  0.3 oz) chopped parsley

SALTY ANCHOVY BUTTER

8 pieces (32 g/1.1 oz) canned
  anchovies, drained
2 cloves garlic, crushed
¼ teaspoon chili powder

NUTRITION FACTS PER SERVING (AVERAGE PER 14 G/½ OZ): Total carbs: 0.5 g | Fiber: 0.1 g | Net carbs: 0.4 g | Protein: 0.2 g | Fat: 9.9 g | Calories: 90 kcal
MACRONUTRIENT RATIO: Calories from carbs (2%), protein (1%), fat (97%)

SWEET BUTTERS

½ cup (113 g/4 oz) softened unsalted butter

PUMPKIN PIE BUTTER

¼ cup (50 g/1.8 oz) pumpkin purée
1 teaspoon pumpkin pie spice
1 tablespoon (10 g/0.4 oz) powdered erythritol or Swerve

MAPLE & PECAN PIE BUTTER

⅓ cup (33 g/1.2 oz) pecans, chopped
½ teaspoon ground cinnamon
2 tablespoons (20 g/0.7 oz) powdered erythritol or Swerve
¼ teaspoon sugar-free maple extract

CHOCOLATE & ORANGE GANACHE BUTTER

2 tablespoons (10 g/0.4 oz) cacao powder
1 teaspoon fresh orange zest
2 tablespoons (20 g/0.7 oz) powdered erythritol or Swerve
⅛ teaspoon sea salt

VANILLA & CINNAMON CREAM BUTTER

½ teaspoon vanilla powder or 1 tablespoon (15 ml) sugar-free vanilla extract
½ teaspoon ground cinnamon
1 tablespoon (10 g/0.4 oz) powdered Erythritol or Swerve

In a medium bowl, mix the softened butter and your preferred spices, herbs, and other ingredients. Spoon the butter onto a piece of parchment paper. Wrap the butter tightly and roll it to create a log shape. Twist the ends of the paper in opposite directions to seal. Store the butter in the fridge for up to a week or freeze for up to 6 months. To freeze it, it helps if you slice it into as many servings as needed. Instead of butter, you can also use ghee or virgin coconut oil (both for sweet and savory butter), and lard or duck fat (for savory butter). If you use butter alternatives, pour the mixture into a silicone ice cube tray and refrigerate: it's perfect for portion control!

NOTE:
Here are some suggestions for how to serve flavored butter: Spread on Speedy Keto Crackers (page 50), use in Harissa Fish Tray Bake (page 100), Thai Curry Chicken Tray Bake (page 102), or with pork chops, fish and seafood, roasted or steamed vegetables, or Cauliflower Rice (page 13). Try sweet butters on top of Chocolate Chip Pancakes (page 42) or use them to make butter or "bullet-proof" coffee.

Homemade Dark Chocolate Three Ways

HANDS-ON TIME: 10 MINUTES
OVERALL TIME: 15 MINUTES + CHILLING

DARK CHOCOLATE USING UNSWEETENED CHOCOLATE

3 ounces (85 g) unsweetened chocolate
3 ounces (85 g) cacao butter
⅓ cup (50 g/1.8 oz) powdered erythritol or Swerve
1 teaspoon sugar-free vanilla extract or ½ teaspoon vanilla powder
Pinch salt
Few drops liquid stevia, to taste (optional)

YIELD: 8 OZ/225 G

Chocoholics, rejoice! You don't have to give up your favorite treat because you're eating keto. Low-carb, sugar-free chocolate is real, and it's just a few simple steps away! This essential recipe even includes a vegan variation.

Melt the unsweetened chocolate and cacao butter in a double boiler, or heatproof bowl placed over a small saucepan filled with 1 cup (240 ml) of water, over medium heat. Remove from the heat and stir in the erythritol or Swerve, vanilla, and salt. If you want a sweeter taste, add the stevia. Pour the chocolate into candy or chocolate molds or onto a parchment-lined baking sheet. Let it harden at room temperature or in the refrigerator. Remove from the molds. Store at room temperature or refrigerate for up to 3 months.

NUTRITION FACTS PER SERVING (28 G/1 OZ): Total carbs: 3 g | Fiber: 1.5 g | Net carbs: 1.5 g | Protein: 1.5 g | Fat: 16.2 g | Calories: 164 kcal
MACRONUTRIENT RATIO: Calories from carbs (4%), protein (4%), fat (92%)

DARK CHOCOLATE USING CACAO POWDER

4 ounces (112 g) cacao butter
½ cup (40 g/1.4 oz) unsweetened cacao powder
⅓ cup (50 g/1.8 oz) powdered erythritol or Swerve
1 teaspoon sugar-free vanilla extract or ½ teaspoon vanilla powder
Pinch salt
Few drops liquid stevia, to taste (optional)

YIELD: 7.5 OZ/213 G

Melt the cacao butter in a double boiler, or heatproof bowl placed over a small saucepan filled with 1 cup (240 ml) of water, over medium heat. Remove from the heat and stir in the cacao powder, erythritol or Swerve, vanilla, and salt. If you want a sweeter taste, add the stevia. Pour into candy or chocolate molds and let harden at room temperature or in the refrigerator. Once hardened, remove from the molds and keep in an airtight container. Store at room temperature or refrigerate for up to 3 months.

NUTRITION FACTS PER SERVING (28 G/1 OZ): Total carbs: 3.5 g | Fiber: 1.8 g | Net carbs: 1.7 g | Protein: 1.1 g | Fat: 15.9 g | Calories: 150 kcal **MACRONUTRIENT RATIO:** Calories from: carbs (4%), protein (3%), fat (93%)

DARK CHOCOLATE USING COCONUT OIL

½ cup (110 g/3.9 oz) coconut oil
½ cup (40 g/1.5 oz) unsweetened cacao powder
¼ cup (40 g/1.4 oz) powdered erythritol or Swerve
1 teaspoon sugar-free vanilla extract or ½ teaspoon vanilla powder
Pinch salt
Few drops liquid stevia, to taste (optional)

YIELD: 6.8 OZ/195 G

Melt the coconut oil in a double boiler, or heatproof bowl placed over a small saucepan filled with 1 cup (240 ml) of water, over medium heat. Remove from the heat and stir in the cacao powder, erythritol or Swerve, vanilla, and salt. If you want a sweeter taste, add the stevia. Pour into candy or chocolate molds and let harden in the refrigerator. Once hardened, remove from the molds and store in an airtight container. Always store in the refrigerator: coconut oil melts at room temperature. Refrigerate for up to 3 months or freeze for up to 6 months.

NUTRITION FACTS PER SERVING (28 G/1 OZ): Total carbs: 3.7 g | Fiber: 1.9 g | Net carbs: 1.8 g | Protein: 1.1 g | Fat: 16.4 g | Calories: 151 kcal **MACRONUTRIENT RATIO:** Calories from: carbs (4%), protein (3%), fat (93%)

BREAKFAST SAUSAGE GUAC STACKS, PAGE 34

ITALIAN SAUSAGE FRITTATA, PAGE 32

CHOCOLATE CHIP PANCAKES, PAGE 42

CHAPTER 2

SATIATING, FAT-FUELED
Breakfasts

CARROT CAKE OATMEAL, PAGE 39

SWEET CINNAMON ROLLS, PAGE 38

BREAKFAST EGG MUFFINS TWO WAYS, PAGE 24

FAT-FUELED SMOOTHIE TWO WAYS, PAGE 43

BREAKFAST IS PROBABLY MY FAVORITE MEAL OF THE DAY.

It involves so many delicious decisions: Sweet or savory? Hot or cold? A leisurely sit-down meal, or a simple treat nibbled alongside a quick cup of coffee or tea?

But breakfast can be tricky when you're following a keto diet. If you don't plan ahead, you're liable either to a) reach for a high-carb option, like a muffin, doughnut, or bagel, when you find yourself in a pinch—and that'll kick you out of ketosis; or b) skip breakfast altogether, and then end up overeating later on.

Neither option is a great idea. Instead, make a healthy breakfast part of each morning with the recipes in this chapter. You don't have to spend a ton of time on it, either. If you make a batch of savory Jalapeño & Cheese Muffins (page 25) or Sweet Cinnamon Rolls (page 38) in advance, you'll have a filling breakfast on hand whether you're at home or running out to school or work. Or, you can whip up a Fat-Fueled Smoothie (page 43) for a full meal in a glass in five minutes. And if you find yourself with a little more time on a weekend morning, you'll want to try the Easy Italian Breakfast Bake on page 37 or the decadent (and kid-friendly!) Chocolate Chip Pancakes on page 42. And all of these recipes are sure to keep cravings at bay until lunchtime—and beyond.

Spanish Eggs

2 SERVINGS
HANDS-ON TIME: 10 MINUTES
OVERALL TIME: 30 MINUTES

2 tablespoons (30 g/1.1 oz) ghee,
   lard, or coconut oil
½ small (30 g/2.1 oz) red onion,
   peeled and sliced
1 clove garlic, crushed
1 medium (120 g/4.2 oz) red pepper,
   seeded and sliced
1 small hot chile pepper
1 cup (240 g/8.5 oz) diced canned
   tomatoes
2 tablespoons (8 g/0.3 oz) chopped
   fresh parsley
Salt and freshly ground black
   pepper, to taste
2 large pastured eggs
Optional: ½ cup (56 g/2 oz) Cheddar
   cheese, grated

Baked eggs get a flavorful Spanish twist (and an impressive presentation!) in this simple breakfast. These Spanish Eggs are great on their own or with Sourdough Keto Buns (page 10), or Keto Tortillas (page 11). And they make a lovely light vegetarian dinner, too.

Preheat the oven to 400°F (200°C, or gas mark 6). Grease a large pan with the ghee, lard, or coconut oil, and add the onion and garlic. Cook until translucent, 3 to 4 minutes, and then add the red pepper and chile pepper. Mix frequently and cook for about 10 minutes.

Stir in the tomatoes and parsley, saving some parsley for garnish. Cook for about a minute. Season with salt and black pepper and take off the heat. Spoon the mixture into two ovenproof dishes. Make a hollow in the middle of the mixture in each dish and crack an egg into each. Top the eggs with grated Cheddar cheese, if you like. Bake in the oven for 15 to 20 minutes.

The eggs are done when the whites are cooked and the yolks are still runny. Remove from the oven, sprinkle with some more chopped parsley, and serve immediately.

NUTRITION FACTS PER SERVING: Total carbs: 10.3 g | Fiber: 4 g | Net carbs: 6.4 g | Protein: 8.3 g | Fat: 20.3 g | Calories: 256 kcal
MACRONUTRIENT RATIO: Calories from carbs (11%), protein (14%), fat (75%)

Eggs Florentine in Portobello Mushrooms

2 SERVINGS
HANDS-ON TIME: 20 MINUTES
OVERALL TIME: 25 MINUTES

2 portobello mushrooms (150 g/
   5.3 oz)

Salt and pepper

1 tablespoon (15 g/0.5 oz) ghee or
   lard

2 large pastured eggs

7.1 ounces (200 g) spinach, fresh or
   cooked

1 recipe Hollandaise Sauce (see
   below)

3.5 ounces (100 g) smoked salmon

HOLLANDAISE SAUCE

⅓ cup (60 g/2.1 oz) butter, ghee, or
   extra-virgin olive oil

2 pastured egg yolks

2 tablespoons (30 ml) fresh lemon
   juice

1 to 2 tablespoons (15 to 30 ml)
   water

½ teaspoon Dijon mustard

Chopped fresh dill, for garnish
   (optional)

Traditional eggs Florentine is naturally low-carb, because it's made with little more than poached eggs, spinach, and hollandaise sauce. But this version is even more nutritious and filling, thanks to the addition of meaty portobello mushrooms and omega-3-packed smoked salmon. Serve it to guests for a luxurious weekend brunch.

Clean the mushrooms with a damp paper towel. Remove the stems and reserve for another use. Season the mushrooms with salt and pepper, and place on a hot pan greased with ghee, bottom-side up. Cook for 1 to 2 minutes, flip them over, and cover the pan. Cook for an additional 5 to 7 minutes, or until tender. Remove from the heat and set aside.

Prepare the poached eggs (see page 23). To prepare fresh spinach, place it in a large pan and cook over medium heat for 1 to 2 minutes, or until wilted, tossing gently with tongs. (If all the spinach doesn't fit into the pan at once, add more spinach to the pan in batches as it cooks down.) Remove from the pan and set aside.

TO MAKE THE HOLLANDAISE SAUCE: Gently melt the butter and set aside; it should be warm, but not too hot (if using olive oil, no heating is needed). Fill a medium saucepan with 1 cup (240 ml) of water and bring to a boil. In a separate bowl, mix the egg yolks with the lemon juice, water, and Dijon mustard. (Use the leftover egg whites to make Sourdough Keto Buns on page 10.) Place the bowl over the saucepan filled with water. The water should not touch the bottom of the bowl. Keep mixing until the sauce starts to thicken. Slowly pour the melted butter into the mixture until thick and creamy, and stir constantly. If the sauce is too thick, add a splash of water. Set aside.

NUTRITION FACTS PER SERVING: Total carbs: 8.4 g | Fiber: 3.2 g | Net carbs: 5.2 g | Protein: 22.9 g | Fat: 44.1 g | Calories: 512 kcal
MACRONUTRIENT RATIO: Calories from carbs (4%), protein (18%), fat (78%)

To serve, place one mushroom, bottom-side up, on each serving plate. Top each with half the wilted spinach (squeeze out any excess water, if necessary), half the smoked salmon, and 1 poached egg. Finally, top with hollandaise sauce, sprinkle with dill, if desired, and serve immediately.

PERFECT EGGS

- I always make eggs ahead of time; they're handy to have at the ready when you don't have time to cook. Toss them into salads or eat with some crispy bacon, smoked salmon, or avocado.
- HARD-BOILED EGGS: Fresh eggs don't peel well. It's better if you use eggs that you bought 7 to 10 days before cooking. Place the eggs in a pot and fill with water, covering them by an inch (2.5 cm). Bring to a boil over high heat. Turn off the heat and cover with a lid. Remove from the burner and keep the eggs covered in the pot (10 to 12 minutes for medium-size eggs; 13 to 14 minutes for large; 15 to 16 minutes for extra-large; 17 to 18 minutes for jumbo and duck eggs). When done, transfer to a bowl filled with ice water and let the eggs sit for 5 minutes. To peel, remove from the ice water and knock each egg several times against the countertop or work surface to crack the shells. Gently peel off the shells. Once cooled, store unpeeled in the fridge for up to a week.
- POACHED EGGS: Fill a medium saucepan with water and a dash of vinegar. Bring to a boil over high heat. Crack each egg individually into a ramekin or a cup. Using a spoon, create a gentle whirlpool in the water; this will help the egg white wrap around the egg yolk. Slowly lower the egg into the water in the center of the whirlpool. Turn off the heat and cook for 3 to 4 minutes. Use a slotted spoon to remove the egg from the water and place it on a plate. Repeat for all remaining eggs. Once cool, place all the eggs in an airtight container filled with cold water and keep refrigerated for up to 5 days. To reheat the eggs, place them in a mug filled with hot tap water for a couple of minutes. This will be enough to warm them up without overcooking.
- FRIED EGGS: Crack the eggs into a large pan greased with some ghee. Cook over medium-high heat until the egg white is opaque and the egg yolk is still runny. As the eggs cook, pour a few tablespoons of the hot fat over the egg whites. Serve immediately. (Fried eggs should not be prepared in advance.)

Breakfast Egg Muffins Two Ways

12 MUFFINS
HANDS-ON TIME: 10 MINUTES
OVERALL TIME: 35 MINUTES

BRIE EGG MUFFINS

2 tablespoons (30 g/1.1 oz) ghee or
   duck fat, divided
2 cloves garlic, minced
2 cups (100 g/3.5 oz) sliced wild
   mushrooms
2 cups (100 g/3.5 oz) chopped kale,
   spinach, or chard
8 large eggs
½ cup (120 g/4.2 oz) ricotta cheese
½ teaspoon sea salt
¼ teaspoon black pepper
5 ounces (142 g) Brie cheese, or blue,
   Swiss, or Cheddar cheese

SAUSAGE-ZUCCHINI EGG MUFFINS

2 tablespoons (30 g/1.1 oz) ghee or
   duck fat, divided
1 medium (100 g/3.5 oz) onion, finely
   chopped
14.1 ounces (400 g) gluten-free
   sausages, casings removed
8 large eggs
½ cup (120 ml) heavy whipping
   cream or coconut milk
½ teaspoon sea salt
¼ teaspoon black pepper
1 medium (150 g/5.3 oz) zucchini, cut
   into 12 slices

A protein-rich breakfast can really help you stay full until lunch-time rolls around, and these Breakfast Egg Muffins are here to help. I like to keep a batch on hand so that I have something healthy to grab when I'm dashing out the door in the morning: that way, I'm never tempted to reach for sugary treats in a pinch.

Preheat the oven to 350°F (175°C, or gas mark 4). Grease a muffin pan with 1 tablespoon (15 g/0.5 oz) of the ghee or duck fat.

TO MAKE THE BRIE EGG MUFFINS: Heat a skillet greased with the remaining ghee over medium heat. Add the garlic and cook for 1 minute. Then add the mushrooms and kale and cook for another 5 minutes, stirring occasionally. When the mushrooms are cooked and the kale is wilted, take off the heat and set aside. In a bowl, whisk the eggs with the ricotta, salt, and pepper. Distribute the cooked mushroom-kale mixture among 12 muffin tins, top each with an equal portion of the egg mixture, and finish each with a slice of Brie cheese. Season with more black pepper and transfer to the oven. Bake for 20 to 25 minutes, or until the muffins are golden brown and puffed up.

TO MAKE THE SAUSAGE-ZUCCHINI EGG MUFFINS: Heat a skillet greased with the remaining 1 tablespoon (15 g/0.5 oz) ghee over medium-high heat. Add the onion and cook for about 5 minutes, until fragrant. Add the sausage meat and cook until browned on all sides, about 5 minutes. Remove from the heat and set aside. In a bowl, whisk the eggs with the cream, salt, and pepper. Distribute the cooked sausage meat between among 12 muffin tins, top each with an equal portion of the egg mixture, and finish each with a slice of zucchini. Season with more black pepper and transfer to the oven. Bake for 20 to 25 minutes, or until the muffins are golden brown and puffed up.

Egg muffins are delicious served warm or cold. Store in the fridge in an airtight container for 4 to 5 days.

NUTRITION FACTS PER MUFFIN: Total carbs: 1.5/1.9 g | Fiber: 0.3/0.3 g | Net carbs: 1.2/1.6 g | Protein: 8.1/9.4 g | Fat: 10.3/20 g | Calories: 132/228 kcal
MACRONUTRIENT RATIO: Calories from carbs (4/3%), protein (25/17%), fat (71/80%)

Jalapeño & Cheese Muffins

12 MUFFINS
HANDS-ON TIME: 10 MINUTES
OVERALL TIME: 40 MINUTES

6 large eggs

⅓ cup (80 ml) extra-virgin olive oil
  or melted butter

¼ cup (60 ml) water

½ teaspoon sea salt

¼ teaspoon black pepper

1 medium (200 g/7.1 oz) zucchini,
  grated

1½ cups (170 g/6 oz) grated Cheddar
  cheese

2 medium (28 g/1 oz) jalapeño
  peppers, finely chopped

1 cup (100 g/3.5 oz) almond flour

⅓ cup (40 g/1.4 oz) coconut flour

4 tablespoons (28 g/1 oz) flax meal

2 teaspoons onion powder

½ teaspoon garlic powder

2 teaspoons gluten-free baking
  powder

Savory, spicy, and laden with plenty of Cheddar cheese, these muffins really overdeliver. They're the perfect on-the-go breakfast, but you can easily toss a few into your backpack or briefcase with a handful of raw veggies for lunch, and they double as a dinnertime side dish, too: they're great with Salisbury Steak with Quick Mash (page 132) or Mexican Chicken Bowls (page 85).

Preheat the oven to 350°F (175°C, or gas mark 4). Crack the eggs into a bowl and beat with the olive oil, water, salt, and pepper. Add all the remaining ingredients and mix until well combined. Spoon the mixture into a silicone muffin pan to make 12 muffins (or use a regular muffin pan greased with a small amount of ghee). Place in the oven and bake for about 30 minutes, until the tops are golden brown and the insides are set and fluffy. Remove from the oven and let cool slightly. While the muffins are still warm, remove them from the muffin pan and place on a cooling rack. To store, place in an airtight container and refrigerate for up to 5 days, or freeze for up to 6 months.

NUTRITION FACTS PER MUFFIN: Total carbs: 4.8 g | Fiber: 2.4 g | Net carbs: 2.4 g | Protein: 9.7 g | Fat: 19 g | Calories: 226 kcal
MACRONUTRIENT RATIO: Calories from carbs (4%), protein (18%), fat (78%)

Abundance Breakfast Bowls

4 SERVINGS
HANDS-ON TIME: 20 MINUTES
OVERALL TIME: 45 MINUTES

CURRIED ZUCCHINI PANCAKES

2 medium (400 g/14.1 oz) zucchini, grated

1 teaspoon salt

2 teaspoons (4 g/0.2 oz) mild curry powder

1 teaspoon onion powder

½ teaspoon ground turmeric

¼ teaspoon black pepper

4 large eggs

3 tablespoons (24 g/0.8 oz) coconut flour

2 tablespoons (8 g/0.3 oz) chopped fresh herbs, such as parsley, cilantro, or mint

2 tablespoons (30 g) duck fat or ghee, divided

SERVE WITH (PER SERVING)

2 pieces (134 g/4.7 oz) gluten-free sausages

1 cup (30 g/1.1 oz) spinach or other soft leafy greens

¼ large (50 g/1.8 oz) avocado, sliced

¼ medium (50 g/1.8 oz) cucumber, sliced

¼ cup (35 g/1.2 oz) kimchi or sauerkraut, drained

1 large egg, soft-boiled, fried, or poached (see page 23)

1 teaspoon sesame seeds

Pinch salt

Pinch red pepper flakes

Here, savory pancakes act as a base for a smorgasbord of healthy, keto-friendly toppings—all of which are super-nutritious. Kimchi (or sauerkraut), for instance, is great for your gut, while avocado is full of healthy fats, and eggs are rich in choline. The result is a perfectly balanced breakfast that'll keep you sated until your next meal.

TO MAKE THE PANCAKES: Combine the zucchini and salt in a large bowl. Let it sit for 20 to 30 minutes, then squeeze out the extra liquid with your hands. Place the drained zucchini into another bowl. After draining, you should end up with about 9.5 ounces (270 g) of zucchini. Add the remaining ingredients, except the duck fat, to the bowl with the drained zucchini and mix until well combined.

Grease a large pan with a tablespoon (15 ml) of the duck fat. Scoop some of the zucchini mixture into a ⅓-cup (80 ml) measuring cup to measure out the pancakes. Place 3 to 4 pancakes at a time in the hot pan, and cook over medium heat for 4 to 5 minutes. Use a spatula to flip them over. Cook for another 2 to 3 minutes, until golden brown. Transfer to a plate, and repeat for the remaining mixture until you've make 8 pancakes, greasing with more ghee as needed.

Once the pancakes are cooked, add the sausages. Cook for 5 to 7 minutes, turning occasionally, until golden brown and cooked through.

Serve the pancakes with the cooked sausages, spinach, avocado, cucumber, kimchi, and egg. Sprinkle with sesame seeds and red pepper flakes. Season with salt to taste, and serve immediately.

NUTRITION FACTS PER SERVING (2 PANCAKES + ALL SERVING OPTIONS): Total carbs: 15 g | Fiber: 7.7 g | Net carbs: 7.3 g | Protein: 38.1 g | Fat: 48.6 g | Calories: 642 kcal
MACRONUTRIENT RATIO: Calories from carbs (5%), protein (25%), fat (70%)

Breakfast Pizza Waffles

4 SERVINGS
HANDS-ON TIME: 15 MINUTES
OVERALL TIME: 25 MINUTES

WAFFLES

3 large pastured eggs

¼ cup (60 g/2.1 oz) cream cheese, at room temperature

⅓ cup (30 g/1.1 oz) grated Parmesan cheese

½ cup (56 g/2 oz) grated Cheddar cheese

3 tablespoons (21 g/0.7 oz) flax meal, or 4 tablespoons (24 g/0.8 oz) almond flour

1 tablespoon (8 g/0.3 oz) coconut flour

1 teaspoon mixed dried Italian herbs (basil, oregano, thyme)

½ teaspoon garlic powder

½ teaspoon onion powder

½ teaspoon gluten-free baking powder

Pinch salt and pepper

TOPPINGS

2 pieces (130 g/4.6 oz) gluten-free sausages

1 teaspoon ghee or duck fat

4 heaped tablespoons (80 g/2.8 oz) Marinara Sauce (page 166)

1 cup (113 g/4 oz) shredded mozzarella cheese

Fresh herbs, such as basil

Pizza for breakfast might sound indulgent, but this low-carb version is actually super-healthy! Make the cheesy waffles in batches and freeze them: then you can just crisp them up in the oven and add your favorite pizza topping before serving.

TO MAKE THE WAFFLES: Place the eggs and cream cheese in a large bowl and mix well. Add the all the remaining ingredients, and mix well. Pour the batter into a preheated waffle maker, close, and cook for 1 to 2 minutes, or until crisp and cooked through. Transfer to a plate and let the waffles cool for a few minutes before serving.

TO PREPARE THE TOPPINGS: Place the sausages on a hot pan lightly greased with ghee. Cook over a medium-high heat until browned on all sides, about 5 to 7 minutes. Remove from the heat, and set aside to cool. Cut the sausages into 1-inch (2.5-cm) pieces.

Place the waffles on a baking tray lined with parchment paper. Preheat the broiler to 400°F (200°C) and crisp up the waffles for 5 minutes. Remove from the oven, and increase the temperature to 430°F (220°C).

Top each waffle with one-fourth of the marinara sauce, shredded mozzarella, and browned sausage pieces. Place under the broiler again and cook for about 3 to 5 minutes, until the cheese is melted and the sausages are lightly crispy. Serve hot. Store any leftover waffles (without toppings) in an airtight container in the fridge for up to 5 days or freeze for up to 3 months.

NOTES:
- To make this meal vegetarian, simply omit the sausages and top with extra cheese, cooked spinach, olives, and/or mushrooms.
- These waffles also make an especially delicious base for a keto-friendly take on eggs Benedict. Just top them with poached eggs and Hollandaise Sauce (page 22)!

NUTRITION FACTS PER SERVING (1 WAFFLE WITH TOPPINGS): Total carbs: 7.4 g | Fiber: 2.3 g | Net carbs: 5.1 g | Protein: 24.7 g | Fat: 37.2 g | Calories: 457 kcal
MACRONUTRIENT RATIO: Calories from carbs (4%), protein (22%), fat (74%)

Green Shakshuka

2 SERVINGS
HANDS-ON TIME: 10 MINUTES
OVERALL TIME: 20 MINUTES

2 tablespoons (30 g/1.1 oz) ghee or
virgin coconut oil
½ small (35 g/1.2 oz) yellow onion,
sliced
1 clove garlic, minced
1 medium (120 g/4.2 oz) green bell
pepper, sliced
1 small (150 g/5.3 oz) zucchini, cut
into ½-inch (1-cm) cubes
½ cup (120 g/4.2 oz) canned
chopped tomatoes
½ teaspoon ground cumin
½ teaspoon paprika
¼ teaspoon ground coriander
⅛ teaspoon cayenne pepper
Salt and pepper, to taste
3 cups (90 g/3.2 oz) fresh spinach
4 large eggs
1 tablespoon (4 g/0.2 oz) chopped
fresh cilantro or parsley
Optional: ⅓ cup (50 g/1.8 oz)
crumbled feta cheese and
1 medium (150 g/5.3 oz) avocado,
sliced

This dish is a one-skillet wonder! Shakshuka is an Arabic dish featuring poached eggs in tomatoes, peppers, and onions, and my take on it is packed with nutritious, low-carb green vegetables, like zucchini, green peppers, and iron-rich spinach, plus a scattering of fresh cilantro. Adding a handful of feta cheese and/or avocado provides healthy fats, and will keep you fuller for even longer, too.

In a large skillet greased with ghee, cook the onion over medium-high heat for 5 to 8 minutes, until lightly browned.

Add the garlic, green pepper, and zucchini. Cook for about 2 minutes, stirring occasionally. Add the tomatoes, cumin, paprika, coriander, cayenne pepper, salt, and black pepper. Cook for about 5 minutes, or until the vegetables are tender. Add the spinach and cook for a minute, until wilted.

Use a spatula to make 4 wells in the mixture. Crack 1 egg into each well and cook until the egg whites are opaque and cooked through and the egg yolks are still runny. Remove from the heat. Garnish with the cilantro, and add the optional feta cheese or avocado on top. Serve immediately, or refrigerate for up to 3 days (without the fried eggs).

NUTRITION FACTS PER SERVING: Total carbs: 12.6 g | Fiber: 4.1 g | Net carbs: 8.5 g | Protein: 16.3 g | Fat: 25.4 g | Calories: 338 kcal
MACRONUTRIENT RATIO: Calories from carbs (10%), protein (20%), fat (70%)

Italian Sausage Frittata

4 SERVINGS
HANDS-ON TIME: 15 MINUTES
OVERALL TIME: 30 MINUTES

2 tablespoons (30 g/1.1 oz) ghee,
  lard, or virgin coconut oil
7.1 ounces (200 g) gluten-free
  Italian-style sausages
2 medium (30 g/1.1 oz) spring onions,
  white and green parts, sliced and
  separated
1 medium (120 g/4.2 oz) red bell
  pepper, sliced
2 cloves garlic, minced
4 ounces (112 g) Swiss chard, stalks
  and leaves separated and roughly
  chopped
8 large eggs
1 teaspoon dried Italian herbs
¼ teaspoon fine sea salt
Ground black pepper
1 cup (113 g/4 oz) grated mozzarella
  cheese, divided
½ cup (45 g/1.6 oz) grated Parmesan
  cheese, divided
½ cup (75 g/2.7 oz) cherry tomatoes,
  halved

Here's another one-dish meal that's basically foolproof. Make this Italian sausage frittata tonight and enjoy it hot or cold tomorrow: it's delicious both ways. And a single slice is an entire meal, because it's stuffed to the gills with Swiss chard, red pepper, tomatoes, sausage, and plenty of cheese.

Grease a large skillet with the ghee. Add the sausages and cook over medium-low heat for 10 to 12 minutes, until browned on all sides and cooked through. Transfer to a plate and set aside. Let them cool slightly and then cut into about 1-inch (2.5-cm) pieces.

Place the white parts of the spring onions in the skillet where you cooked the sausages and cook for 2 to 3 minutes, stirring frequently. Add the red pepper, garlic, and chard stalks. Cook for 3 minutes, stirring frequently. Add the chard leaves and cook for 1 minute.

Preheat the broiler. In a large bowl, lightly beat the eggs with the herbs, salt, and pepper. Add the mozzarella and Parmesan cheese (reserve some cheese for topping). Pour the eggs into the skillet. Cook over low heat until the top starts to firm up and the edges are turning opaque, 8 to 10 minutes. Top with the reserved cheese, browned sausages, cherry tomatoes, and green parts of the spring onions. Place under the broiler for about 5 minutes to crisp up the top. Let the frittata cool slightly and cut it into 4 pieces. Serve immediately or let it cool and refrigerate for up to 4 days, or freeze for up to 3 months.

NUTRITION FACTS PER SERVING (¼ FRITTATA): Total carbs: 7.4 g | Fiber: 1.9 g | Net carbs: 5.5 g | Protein: 33.4 g | Fat: 34.7 g | Calories: 479 kcal
MACRONUTRIENT RATIO: Calories from carbs (5%), protein (28%), fat (67%)

Breakfast Sausage Guac Stacks

2 SERVINGS
HANDS-ON TIME: 10 MINUTES
OVERALL TIME: 15 MINUTES

QUICK GUACAMOLE

1 medium (150 g/5.3 oz) avocado
½ small (35 g/1.2 oz) white or yellow onion, chopped
2 tablespoons (30 ml) fresh lime juice
Salt and pepper, to taste

SAUSAGE STACKS

1 to 2 tablespoons (15 to 30 g/0.5 to 1.1 oz) ghee, divided
6 ounces (170 g) gluten-free sausage meat
2 large pastured eggs
Salt and pepper, to taste

Healthy low-carb eating really doesn't have to be complicated, and this electrolyte-rich breakfast meal is proof. Top homemade sausage patties with a zesty, two-minute guacamole, and add a fried egg for additional protein. It's a perfect example of a fuss-free keto breakfast. No wonder it went viral over social media!

TO MAKE THE GUACAMOLE: Halve the avocado and scoop into a bowl. Add the onion, lime juice, salt, and pepper. Mash with a fork and set aside.

TO MAKE THE SAUSAGE STACKS: Heat a pan greased with half of the ghee over medium heat. Using your hands, shape the sausage meat into small patties. Place on the pan and cook undisturbed for 2 to 3 minutes. Flip over and cook for 1 to 2 more minutes more. Set aside.

Grease the pan with the remaining ghee and crack in the eggs. Cook until the egg whites are cooked through and the egg yolks are still runny (using an egg mold, if you like).

Top each sausage patty with the prepared guacamole and fried egg. Season with salt and pepper to taste, and eat immediately.

NOTES:
- You can prepare the guacamole and fry the sausage patties in advance. Keep them in an airtight container for up to 3 days. Serve with fried or poached eggs (see page 23).
- Looking for a vegetarian option? Try with pan-roasted portobello mushrooms instead of the sausage!

NUTRITION FACTS PER SERVING (1 STACK): Total carbs: 9.9 g | Fiber: 5.5 g | Net carbs: 4.4 g | Protein: 20.1 g | Fat: 43.9 g | Calories: 509 kcal
MACRONUTRIENT RATIO: Calories from carbs (4%), protein (16%), fat (80%)

Greek Breakfast Hash

2 SERVINGS
HANDS-ON TIME: 15 MINUTES
OVERALL TIME: 25 MINUTES

1 medium (250 g/8.8 oz) eggplant

1 package (125 g/4.4 oz) Halloumi

1 clove garlic, peeled and finely chopped

2 tablespoons (30 g/1.1 oz) ghee or lard

1 teaspoon dried oregano

2 tablespoons (30 ml) extra-virgin olive oil

1 teaspoon balsamic vinegar

Optional: 2 to 4 large pastured eggs

If you're like me, you're already addicted to salty, chewy Halloumi cheese. It's a natural partner for eggplant: both turn up in plenty of traditional Greek dishes, and, happily, they're both low in carbs. If you practice intermittent fasting, add a fried egg or two to this vegetarian hash for a dose of protein, and you've got a savory breakfast with serious staying power.

Roughly dice the eggplant and the Halloumi into 1-inch (2.5-cm) pieces. Cook the garlic in a large pan greased with ghee over medium heat for 1 minute, until fragrant. Add the Halloumi and cook for 5 to 8 minutes, until browned on both sides. Add the diced eggplant and oregano, and cook for another 5 minutes. Stir, cover, and cook for 5 more minutes, or until the eggplant is soft. Remove from the heat and set aside.

Mix the olive oil and balsamic vinegar in a small bowl. Place the cooked eggplant and Halloumi hash on serving plates. Drizzle with the olive oil and balsamic vinegar mixture. Optionally, serve with fried eggs (see page 23).

NUTRITION FACTS PER SERVING: Total carbs: 10.2 g | Fiber: 4.2 g | Net carbs: 6 g | Protein: 13.9 g | Fat: 45.7 g | Calories: 500 kcal
MACRONUTRIENT RATIO: Calories from carbs (5%), protein (11%), fat (84%)

Chorizo & Kale Hash

2 SERVINGS
HANDS-ON TIME: 10 MINUTES
OVERALL TIME: 25 MINUTES

- 1 package (300 g/10.6 oz) dark-leaf kale
- 1 small (100 g/3.5 oz) rutabaga
- 2 tablespoons (30 g/1.1 oz) ghee or lard
- 1 medium (60 g/2.1 oz) red onion, finely chopped
- 7.1 ounces (200 g) ground pork
- 2 ounces (56 g) Spanish chorizo or pepperoni, sliced
- Salt and freshly ground black pepper, to taste
- Optional: Fried pastured eggs or sliced avocado

Low-carb, nutrient-dense leafy greens are a keto staple, and they're delicious in just about any savory meal. And they're the perfect foil for chorizo's lively flavor in this breakfast hash (which, incidentally, moonlights as a dinnertime side dish: try serving it alongside roast meat). Top with a poached egg for extra protein—not to mention choline and omega-3s.

Wash and tear the kale into 2-inch (5-cm) pieces. Peel and dice the rutabaga or use a julienne peeler to create thin "noodles."

Grease a large pan with ghee and place over medium-high heat. When the pan is hot, toss in the onion. Cook for just about 3 minutes. When the onion is lightly browned, add the pork and cook for about 5 minutes, stirring frequently. Next, add the kale and rutabaga, and cook for 10 to 15 minutes. Stir often to avoid burning.

Meanwhile, cook the chorizo in a separate pan until crispy. Add the chorizo and the juices to the pan with the kale when done. Season with salt and black pepper. Serve immediately.

NUTRITION FACTS PER SERVING: Total carbs: 13.7 g | Fiber: 6.3 g | Net carbs: 7.4 g | Protein: 29.8 g | Fat: 49.6 g | Calories: 608 kcal
MACRONUTRIENT RATIO: Calories from carbs (5%), protein (20%), fat (75%)

Easy Italian Breakfast Bake

4 SERVINGS
HANDS-ON TIME: 10 MINUTES
OVERALL TIME: 30 MINUTES

1 tablespoon (15 g/0.5 oz) ghee or
   duck fat
10.6 ounces (300 g) gluten-free
   Italian-style sausages, casings
   removed
⅔ cup (160 g/5.6 oz) Marinara Sauce
   (page 166)
1½ cups (170 g/6 oz) shredded
   mozzarella
7.1 ounces (200 g) broccoli florets or
   broccolini
¼ cup (20 g/0.7 oz) grated Parmesan
   cheese

Think of this six-ingredient breakfast bake as a low-carb take on traditional lasagna. This layered bake features vitamins C- and K-rich broccoli, Italian sausage, and plenty of gooey mozzarella cheese. Serve it to guests for an impromptu Sunday brunch, or do what I do—make it ahead of time for weekday breakfasts, then sit on my hands to keep myself from eating it for three meals a day.

Preheat the oven to 360°F (180°C, or gas mark 4). Heat a skillet greased with the ghee over medium-high heat. Add the sausage and cook for 3 to 5 minutes, until browned on all sides. Add about half of the marinara sauce to the skillet and remove from the heat. Distribute the sausage-marinara mixture evenly among 4 mini baking dishes (or use one regular-size dish).

Top with half of the mozzarella, the broccoli florets, and the remaining marinara sauce. Top with the remaining mozzarella and sprinkle with the Parmesan. Place in the oven and bake for about 20 minutes. Serve warm, or let cool and refrigerate for up to 4 days.

NUTRITION FACTS PER SERVING: Total carbs: 7.9 g | Fiber: 1.8 g | Net carbs: 6.1 g | Protein: 25.3 g | Fat: 43.7 g | Calories: 526 kcal
MACRONUTRIENT RATIO: Calories from carbs (5%), protein (20%), fat (75%)

Sweet Cinnamon Rolls

10 ROLLS
HANDS-ON TIME: 20 MINUTES
OVERALL TIME: 1 HOUR

DOUGH

2 cups (200 g/7.1 oz) almond flour

⅓ cup (40 g/1.4 oz) coconut flour

¼ cup (25 g/0.9 oz) whey protein or
   egg white protein powder, vanilla or
   unflavored or more almond flour

⅔ cup (80 g/2.8 oz) psyllium husk powder

½ cup (80 g/2.8 oz) powdered erythritol
   or Swerve

15 to 20 drops liquid stevia

¼ teaspoon salt

1 teaspoon baking soda

2 teaspoons cream of tartar

2 large pastured eggs

6 large pastured egg whites

1¼ cups (300 ml) hot water

FILLING

2 tablespoons (30 g/1.1 oz) coconut
   oil, ghee, or butter, softened but not
   melted

1 tablespoon (8 g) ground cinnamon

¼ cup (40 g/1.4 oz) erythritol or Swerve

Pinch salt

ICING

⅓ cup (80 g/2.8 oz) coconut butter,
   melted

1 tablespoon (15 g/0.5 oz) virgin coconut
   oil, melted

Optional: 10 to 15 drops liquid stevia or
   2 tablespoons (20 g/0.7 oz) powdered
   erythritol or Swerve

Traditional cinnamon rolls are high-carb diet disasters. But never fear: My keto version gets the green light. In fact, it's even good for you! Grab one for a quick breakfast or enjoy one as a satisfying dessert.

Preheat the oven to 325°F (165°C, or gas mark 3).

TO MAKE THE DOUGH: Place the almond flour, coconut flour, protein powder, and psyllium husk powder into a mixer. (Note: Don't use whole psyllium husks; run them through a blender if necessary.) Add the powdered erythritol, stevia, salt, baking soda, and cream of tartar, and mix until well combined. Add the eggs and egg whites and process well. Pour in the hot water and process until well combined.

Lay out a sheet of parchment paper or foil on a flat work surface. Transfer the dough to the parchment paper and flatten with your hands. Place the dough on the parchment paper on a flat work surface and set another piece of parchment or foil on top. Roll the dough out until about ½ inch (1.3-cm) thick and a rectangular shape. The sides should be about 14 inches (36 cm) long.

TO MAKE THE FILLING: Mix the softened coconut oil, cinnamon, erythritol, and salt in a bowl until creamy.

Spread the cinnamon filling over the dough, leaving a ½- to 1-inch (1.3- to 2.5-cm) space along each side. Roll up the dough and cut it in half. Then cut each half into 5 pieces to create 10 equal servings.

Place all the rolls cut-side down on a large baking tray except the first and last slices: set these cut-side up. Transfer the tray to the oven and bake for about 40 minutes. When done, remove the tray from the oven and leave the cinnamon rolls to cool.

TO MAKE THE ICING: Mix the melted coconut butter with the coconut oil in a bowl. Optionally, add stevia or erythritol, and mix well. Drizzle the coconut butter mixture over the cooled rolls. Store in a cool place for up to 3 days or in the fridge for up to a week.

NUTRITION FACTS PER ROLL: Total carbs: 14.7 g | Fiber: 10.4 g | Net carbs: 4.4 g | Protein: 7.7 g | Fat: 19.6 g | Calories: 320 kcal
MACRONUTRIENT RATIO: Calories from carbs (8%), protein (14%), fat (78%)

Carrot Cake Oatmeal

6 SERVINGS
HANDS-ON TIME: 10 MINUTES
OVERALL TIME: 3 TO 4 HOURS

¼ cup (55 g/1.9 oz) virgin coconut oil

2 cups (480 ml) unsweetened almond milk or cashew milk

1 cup (240 ml) coconut milk

½ cup (100 g/3.5 oz) unsweetened pumpkin purée

⅓ cup (83 g/2.9 oz) almond butter or coconut butter

½ cup (38 g/1.3 oz) unsweetened shredded coconut

1 cup (110 g/3.9 oz) grated carrot

½ cup (58 g/2 oz) chopped walnuts or pecans

3 tablespoons (30 g/1.1 oz) granulated erythritol or Swerve

1 teaspoon fresh lemon or orange zest

½ teaspoon vanilla powder or 2 teaspoons sugar-free vanilla extract

1 tablespoon (8 g/0.3 oz) pumpkin pie spice

¼ cup (38 g/1.3 oz) chia seeds

Optional: Few drops of liquid stevia

OPTIONAL TOPPINGS

Creamed coconut milk, heavy whipping cream, or mascarpone cheese

Toasted flaked almonds or coconut

Roughly chopped pecan or walnut pieces

I can't imagine a better cool-weather breakfast than this warming, filling, grain-free oatmeal. It's spiked with fragrant autumn spices, and gets a hefty dose of beta-carotene from bright-orange carrot and pumpkin. And thanks to almond butter, coconut, walnuts, and chia seeds, it's big on good fats. This is breakfast-time comfort food at its best!

Preheat the slow cooker. Place all the ingredients apart from the chia seeds in the slow cooker, and heat through for about 1 hour. When the mixture is warm, add the chia seeds and combine well. Cover with a lid and cook on low for 3 to 4 hours, stirring once or twice. When done, taste and add stevia if needed. Serve warm or cold with any optional toppings. To store, let it cool, and place in an airtight container. Store in the fridge for up to 5 days.

NUTRITION FACTS PER SERVING (¾ CUP/180 G/6.4 OZ): Total carbs: 13.9 g | Fiber: 7.5 g | Net carbs: 6.4 g | Protein: 8.2 g | Fat: 34.3 g | Calories: 389 kcal
MACRONUTRIENT RATIO: Calories from carbs (7%), protein (9%), fat (84%)

"No-Tella" Granola

14 SERVINGS
HANDS-ON TIME: 5 MINUTES
OVERALL TIME: 30 MINUTES

2 cups (270 g/9.5 oz) hazelnuts

1 cup (143 g/5 oz) almonds

1 cup (75 g/2.7 oz) unsweetened
 shredded coconut

1½ cups (90 g/3.2 oz) unsweetened
 flaked coconut

¼ cup (38 g/1.3 oz) chia seeds

¼ cup (22 g/0.8 oz) cacao powder
 or unsweetened Dutch process
 cocoa powder

⅓ cup (67 g/2.4 oz) granulated
 erythritol or Swerve

1 teaspoon vanilla powder or
 1 tablespoon (15 ml) unsweetened
 vanilla extract

¼ teaspoon sea salt

¼ cup (60 ml) melted virgin coconut
 oil or ghee

1 large pastured egg white, lightly
 beaten

1 cup (180 g/6.4 oz) 90% dark
 chocolate chips (use at least 85%)

Coconut milk, unsweetened almond
 milk, cream, full-fat yogurt, or sour
 cream, for serving

This crunchy, satisfying, low-carb granola tastes just like the popular chocolate-hazelnut treat. It's got all of the flavor minus the unhealthy additives and sugar. I use low-carb sweetener here, but if you prefer to steer clear of sweeteners, go ahead and skip them altogether: the result will be just as delicious.

Preheat the oven to 350°F (175°C). Roughly chop about half of the hazelnuts and almonds. Place all the dry ingredients—the hazelnuts through the salt, including the liquid vanilla extract, if using—in a mixing bowl and combine well. Add the melted coconut oil and egg white. Mix well until the mixture resembles a crumbly dough.

Transfer the mixture to a baking sheet lined with parchment paper. Bake for 25 minutes, turning halfway through. Remove from the oven and let cool. When the granola has reached room temperature, add the dark chocolate chips and transfer to a glass container. Serve with coconut milk, almond milk, cream, yogurt, or sour cream.

NUTRITION FACTS PER SERVING (½ CUP/70 G/2.5 OZ): Total carbs: 13 g | Fiber: 7.4 g | Net carbs: 5.6 g | Protein: 8.9 g | Fat: 33.9 g | Calories: 369 kcal
MACRONUTRIENT RATIO: Calories from carbs (6%), protein (10%), fat (84%)

Fluffy Cocoa & Berry Omelet

1 SERVING
HANDS-ON TIME: 10 MINUTES
OVERALL TIME: 15 MINUTES

2 tablespoons (20 g/0.7 oz) powdered erythritol or Swerve

3 large pastured eggs

¼ teaspoon cream of tartar

Optional: 5 to 10 drops liquid stevia

1 tablespoon (5 g/0.2 oz) cacao powder

⅓ cup (50 g/1.8 oz) mixed berries (strawberries, raspberries, blueberries, or blackberries)

1 tablespoon (15 g/0.5 oz) ghee or coconut oil

Optional: Dollop of whipped cream, sour cream, or creamed coconut milk

If you've never tried a sweet omelet before, this Fluffy Cocoa & Berry Omelet is the perfect place to start. It's chocolaty but feather-light, and studding it with your favorite berries (which are naturally low in carbs) adds extra color and flavor. Treat yourself to one on a weekend morning.

Set the oven to broil at 480°F (250°C, or gas mark 10). To ensure that the omelet has a smooth texture, place the erythritol into a blender and pulse until powdered.

Separate the egg whites from the yolks. Put the egg yolks into a bowl and set aside. Using an electric mixer or a hand whisk, start whisking the egg whites and add the cream of tartar as you go. Add in the erythritol, liquid stevia (if using), and cacao powder and beat until the egg whites create soft peaks.

In another bowl, mix the egg yolks with a fork and then gently fold in the egg whites. Mix gently so you don't deflate the egg mixture.

Meanwhile, wash the berries and pat them dry. Grease a hot oven-proof pan with ghee, pour in the omelet mixture, and then sprinkle with the berries. Cook over low heat for about 5 minutes, until the bottom of the omelet starts to brown. At that point, remove from the stovetop and place in the oven under the broiler for about 5 minutes.

When done, the top should be slightly brown and crispy while the inside is still soft. Optionally, top with whipped cream, sour cream, or creamed coconut milk.

NUTRITION FACTS PER SERVING: Total carbs: 10 g | Fiber: 2.8 g | Net carbs: 7.2 g | Protein: 20.3 g | Fat: 30 g | Calories: 383 kcal

MACRONUTRIENT RATIO: Calories from carbs (8%), protein (21%), fat (71%)

Chocolate Chip Pancakes

4 SERVINGS (8 MINI PANCAKES)
HANDS-ON TIME: 15 MINUTES
OVERALL TIME: 20 MINUTES

4 large pastured eggs

¼ cup (55 g/1.9 oz) virgin coconut oil or ghee, melted and divided

2 tablespoons (20 g/0.7 oz) granulated erythritol or Swerve

1 cup (100 g/3.5 oz) almond flour

½ teaspoon ground cinnamon or vanilla powder

1 teaspoon cream of tartar or apple cider vinegar

½ teaspoon baking soda

¼ cup (45 g/1.6 oz) dark chocolate chips (85% cacao or more) or roughly chopped dark chocolate

Kids and grown-ups alike adore chocolate chip pancakes, and the good news is that you don't have to give them up just because you're following a keto lifestyle! Here, the ultimate breakfast treat—perfect for birthdays, holidays, and lazy weekend mornings—gets a low-carb makeover.

Crack the eggs into a bowl. Pour in the melted coconut oil, but reserve a small amount for greasing the pan. Whisk well. In another bowl, combine erythritol, almond, flour, cinnamon, cream of tartar or vinegar, and baking soda. Add the dry ingredients to the bowl with the eggs and mix well again. Stir in the dark chocolate chips.

Grease a large pan with the remaining coconut oil and heat over medium heat. Using a spoon or ladle, create 8 small pancakes. (You can use pancake molds to create perfect shapes.) Lower the heat and cook for 3 to 5 minutes, or until the tops of the pancakes start to firm up.

Flip the pancakes over and cook for an additional minute. Place the pancakes on a plate and keep warm in the oven until you've used up all the batter. Serve with butter, full-fat yogurt, or coconut cream.

Store leftover pancakes in an airtight container in the fridge for up to 5 days, or freeze for up to 3 months.

NOTE:
Make this recipe nut-free by substituting ⅓ cup (40 g/1.4 oz) coconut flour for the 1 cup (100 g/3.5 oz) almond flour. If the batter is too thick, add 1 more egg.

NUTRITION FACTS PER SERVING (2 MINI PANCAKES): Total carbs: 8.8 g | Fiber: 3.5 g | Net carbs: 5.3 g | Protein: 12.9 g | Fat: 40.4 g | Calories: 432 kcal
MACRONUTRIENT RATIO: Calories from carbs (5%), protein (12%), fat (83%)

Fat-Fueled Smoothie Two Ways

1 SERVING
HANDS-ON TIME: 5 MINUTES
OVERALL TIME: 5 MINUTES

BASE INGREDIENTS

½ large (100 g/3.5 oz) avocado

¼ cup (60 ml) coconut milk

¾ to 1 cup (180 to 240 ml) water,
plus a few ice cubes

Optional: Liquid stevia powdered
erythritol, or Swerve

FOR A CHOCOLATE SMOOTHIE

1 tablespoon (16 g/0.6 oz) coconut
butter or almond butter

1 tablespoon (5 g/0.2 oz)
unsweetened cocoa powder or
raw cacao

½ teaspoon ground cinnamon

FOR A BERRY SMOOTHIE

½ cup (75 g/2.6 oz) fresh or frozen
berries (raspberries, blackberries,
or strawberries)

¼ teaspoon vanilla powder or
½ teaspoon unsweetened vanilla
extract

Endlessly versatile and so quick to make, keto smoothies like this one are just the thing for busy weekday mornings—or for warm summer days when you can't stand the thought of turning on the stove to cook breakfast. Feel free to get creative with them, too: check out my suggestions for delicious, health-boosting variations below.

Place all the base and flavor-specific ingredients in a blender, including the sweetener (if using). Pulse until smooth. Serve immediately.

VARIATIONS:

Get creative and add any of these ingredients to my basic Fat-Fueled Smoothie.

- 1 tablespoon (15 ml) MCT oil gives you an extra energy boost.
- 2 tablespoons (15 g/0.5 oz) collagen powder or 1 scoop quality protein powder helps you stay full for longer.
- 1 cup (30 g/1.1 oz) fresh spinach is a great way to sneak more greens into your diet!
- 1 tablespoon (8 g/0.3 oz) chia seeds adds fiber and produces a thicker texture.
- 1 to 2 tablespoons (16 to 32 g/0.6 to 1.1 oz) of any nut or seed butter, or coconut butter, contributes a creamy texture, plus fiber, protein, and healthy fats.
- 1 to 2 teaspoons maca powder boosts energy levels, strengthens your immune system, and increases stamina and libido. It's also high in phytochemicals. Maca is also a powerful adaptogen, that is, it helps our bodies adapt to—and avoid damage from—environmental factors such as stress, poor diet, and toxins.

NUTRITION FACTS PER SERVING (CHOCOLATE SMOOTHIE): Total carbs: 17.7 g | Fiber: 11.6 g | Net carbs: 6.1 g | Protein: 5.2 g | Fat: 36.3 g | Calories: 377 kcal
MACRONUTRIENT RATIO: Calories from carbs (6%), protein (6%), Fat (88%)

NUTRITION FACTS PER SERVING (BERRY SMOOTHIE): Total carbs: 16.4 g | Fiber: 8.8 g | Net carbs: 7.6 g | Protein: 3.9 g | Fat: 27 g | Calories: 301 kcal
MACRONUTRIENT RATIO: Calories from carbs (10%), protein (5%), fat (85%)

SPEEDY KETO CRACKERS, PAGE 50

SOUTHERN DUCK DEVILED EGGS, PAGE 48

HAM AND CHEESE
FAT BOMBS, PAGE 46

CHAPTER 3

SATISFYING KETO
Snacks and Appetizers

BAKED JALAPEÑO POPPER DIP, PAGE 51

PERI PERI ROASTED NUTS, PAGE 49

CRISPY RANCH CHICKEN WINGS, PAGE 53

AVOCADO-EGG STUFFED
BACON CUPS, PAGE 47

ONCE YOU'VE GOT A FILLING, FAT-FUELED BREAK-FAST UNDER YOUR BELT, you'll usually find that you're pretty well set until lunch. You're less likely to feel hungry or to crave high-carb snacks. But let's face it: on busy days you might not get around to lunch until late afternoon, and on other days you may just feel hungrier than usual.

That's okay: this chapter has you covered. I've created lots of nutritious, low-carb snacks that will see you safely through those hungry hours. Many of them make great party snacks, too: even your non-keto guests will be begging for the recipes! Take the Baked Jalapeño Popper Dip on page 51, for instance: serve it at your next shindig along with drinks and keto crackers, and no one will know (or care!) that it's low-carb. Same goes for the Crispy Ranch Chicken Wings on page 53: they're serious crowd-pleasers.

Cooking for just yourself? Treat yourself to the Ham and Cheese Fat Bombs on page 46, which make great late-morning or midafternoon snacks (or can even stand in for a light lunch), or make a batch of the Southern Duck Deviled Eggs on page 48. All of them are sure to keep you going until your next meal.

Ham and Cheese Fat Bombs

6 FAT BOMBS
HANDS-ON TIME: 15 MINUTES
OVERALL TIME: 15 MINUTES +
CHILLING TIME

3.5 ounces (100 g) full-fat cream
   cheese, at room temperature
¼ cup (56 g/2 oz) unsalted butter, at
   room temperature
¼ cup (30 g/1.1 oz) grated Cheddar
   cheese or Gouda cheese
2 tablespoons (10 g/0.4 oz) chopped
   fresh basil
Pepper, to taste
6 slices (90 g/3.2 oz) Parma ham
6 large (30 g/1.1 oz) green olives,
   pitted
6 basil leaves

Wrapped in sweet-and-salty Parma ham, these savory fat bombs are proof that good things come in small packages. And if you're practicing intermittent fasting, fat bombs are especially handy. Why? If you're eating twice a day, you'll need fewer high-fat meals to supply your energy needs, so the best way to enjoy fat bombs like these is as a high-fat treat with or after a meal.

In a bowl, mash together the cream cheese and butter, or process in a food processor until smooth.

Add the Cheddar cheese and chopped basil. Mix until well combined. Season with pepper. Refrigerate for 20 to 30 minutes, or until set.

Using a large spoon or an ice-cream scoop, divide the mixture into 6 balls. Wrap each ball in 1 slice of Parma ham and place on a plate. Top each ball with 1 olive and 1 basil leaf and pierce with a toothpick to hold it in place. Enjoy immediately or refrigerate in an airtight container for up to 5 days.

NUTRITION FACTS PER SERVING (1 FAT BOMB): Total carbs: 0.9 g | Fiber: 0.2 g | Net carbs: 0.7 g | Protein: 6.4 g | Fat: 16.4 g | Calories: 167 kcal
MACRONUTRIENT RATIO: Calories from carbs (2%), protein (14%), fat (84%)

Avocado-Egg Stuffed Bacon Cups

6 SERVINGS
HANDS-ON TIME: 25 MINUTES
OVERALL TIME: 40 MINUTES

12 large (450 g/1 lb) slices bacon

4 large eggs, hard-boiled and diced
(see page 23)

2 tablespoons (30 g/1.1 oz)
Mayonnaise (page 163)

2 tablespoon (30 ml) fresh lemon
juice

1 tablespoon (4 g/0.2 oz) chopped
fresh parsley

1 tablespoon (4 g/0.2 oz) chopped
fresh dill

Salt and pepper, to taste

2 medium (300 g/oz) avocados,
peeled, pitted, and chopped

Everything tastes better with bacon. Fact. And these fun-to-make bacon cups are a simple but impressive way to turn an herbed blend of egg and avocado into a satisfying snack or a tempting party hors d'oeuvre with plenty of crunch and flavor—not to mention healthy fats.

Preheat the oven to 300°F (150°C, or gas mark 2) and place a muffin tin upside down on a baking sheet lined with aluminum foil.

Cut 6 slices of the bacon in half to make 12 smaller pieces. Lay 2 bacon pieces in a cross shape over 6 of the upturned muffin cups. Then wrap a whole slice of bacon around each muffin cup, covering the outsides of the cross. Repeat with the remaining bacon to create 6 bacon cups. Transfer to the oven and bake for 25 to 30 minutes, or until crispy. Remove the muffin tray from the oven and let the bacon cool on the tin. (You can strain and reserve the bacon grease and use it for cooking.)

Meanwhile, prepare the avocado-egg salad. Place the diced eggs, mayonnaise, lemon juice, parsley, and dill in a mixing bowl. Combine well, and season with salt and pepper. Add the avocados and mix again. (You can mash part of the avocado with a fork for a creamy consistency, if you like, or mix gently and leave the mixture chunky.)

To serve, fill each bacon cup with the avocado-egg salad. Serve immediately or store the bacon and the egg filling separately in the fridge for up to 2 days.

NUTRITION FACTS PER SERVING (1 STUFFED BACON CUP): Total carbs: 4.9 g | Fiber: 3.4 g | Net carbs: 1.5 g | Protein: 15.5 g | Fat: 18.1 g | Calories: 238 kcal
MACRONUTRIENT RATIO: Calories from carbs (3%), protein (27%), fat (70%)

Southern Duck Deviled Eggs

4 SERVINGS
HANDS-ON TIME: 10 MINUTES
OVERALL TIME: 20 MINUTES

4 duck eggs or jumbo chicken eggs
1 medium (40 g/1.4 oz) pickle
¼ cup (55 g/1.9 oz) Mayonnaise (page 163)
1 teaspoon Dijon mustard
1 tablespoon (15 ml) pickle juice or fresh lemon juice
Salt and pepper, to taste
1 tablespoon (10 g/0.3 oz) diced red bell pepper
Pinch paprika

Deviled eggs are another staple of just about every keto kitchen. That's because they're easy to make—and even easier to grab when cravings strike. (And everyone loves them, even if they're not following a keto lifestyle.) But these aren't your run-of-the-mill deviled eggs: this version is made with duck eggs, which have a stronger flavor than chicken eggs, and they're especially filling.

First, hard-boil the eggs by following the instructions on page 23. Cut the eggs in half and carefully—without breaking the egg whites—spoon the egg yolks into a bowl. Set the whites aside.

Finely chop or slice the pickle, and reserve some for garnish. Add the mayonnaise, Dijon mustard, pickle juice, and pickles to the bowl with the egg yolks. Mix until well combined with a fork, and season with salt and pepper to taste.

Use a spoon or a small cookie scoop to fill the egg white halves with the egg yolk mixture. Garnish with the reserved pickles, red pepper, and paprika. Serve, or place in an airtight container and refrigerate for up to 2 days.

NUTRITION FACTS PER SERVING (2 DEVILED EGGS): Total carbs: 1.9 g | Fiber: 0.3 g | Net carbs: 1.6 g | Protein: 9.3 g | Fat: 21.1 g | Calories: 235 kcal
MACRONUTRIENT RATIO: Calories from carbs (3%), protein (16%), fat (81%)

Peri Peri Roasted Nuts

8 SERVINGS
HANDS-ON TIME: 5 MINUTES
OVERALL TIME: 20 MINUTES

1½ cups (210 g/7.4 oz) almonds
1½ cups (200 g/7.1 oz) macadamia
  nuts
½ cup (70 g/2.5 oz) cashews
1 tablespoon (7 g/0.3 oz) paprika
1 teaspoon onion powder
1 teaspoon sea salt
½ teaspoon garlic powder
½ teaspoon dried parsley
½ teaspoon dried oregano
½ teaspoon chile powder
¼ teaspoon ground coriander
¼ teaspoon ground cumin
¼ teaspoon black pepper
⅛ teaspoon nutmeg
⅛ teaspoon cayenne pepper
1 tablespoon (15 g/0.5 oz)
  unsweetened tomato paste
2 tablespoons (30 ml) extra-virgin
  olive oil
Optional: 1 tablespoon (10 g/
  0.4 oz) erythritol or Swerve, or
  3 to 5 drops liquid stevia

This recipe for this spicy nut mix was inspired by a famous appetizer from a British restaurant chain called Nando's. The original recipe is full of sugar, so it's not keto-friendly, but I once made a promise to a friend that I'd come up with a low-carb version—and here it is! You can skip the low-carb sweetener, if you like, but it does make them taste authentic.

Preheat the oven to 350°F (175°C, or gas mark 4). Place the nuts, preferably activated (see Note below), in a mixing bowl. Add all the remaining ingredients. (If using stevia, mix it with the olive oil before adding it to the nuts.) Mix until well combined and all the nuts are coated with the spice mixture.

Spread the nuts in a single layer on a baking sheet lined with parchment paper. Roast for 8 to 12 minutes, mixing the nuts with a spatula halfway through. Remove from the oven and let cool. Store in an airtight container for up to 1 month.

NOTE:
Activated nuts and seeds are more easily digested, and their nutrients are better absorbed. Plus, activating makes them deliciously crunchy. To do this, place the nuts or seeds in a bowl filled with water or salted water, ensuring that the nuts are completely submerged. Leave at room temperature overnight. Drain and spread on a parchment-lined baking sheet. Place in the oven and dry at a low temperature, about 150°F (65°C), for 6 to 12 hours, or until completely dry, turning occasionally. Or dry nuts in a dehydrator for 12 to 24 hours, turning occasionally, until completely dry. Store activated nuts and seeds in an airtight container.

NUTRITION FACTS PER SERVING (⅓ CUP/40 G/1.4 OZ): Total carbs: 13.3 g | Fiber: 6.4 g | Net carbs: 6.9 g | Protein: 9.6 g | Fat: 39.8 g | Calories: 421 kcal
MACRONUTRIENT RATIO: Calories from carbs (6%), protein (9%), fat (85%)

Speedy Keto Crackers

12 SERVINGS (24 CRACKERS)
HANDS-ON TIME: 10 MINUTES
OVERALL TIME: 30 MINUTES

¼ cup (36 g/1.3 oz) sesame seeds

¼ cup (32 g/1.1 oz) pumpkin seeds

¼ cup (38 g/1.3 oz) chia seeds

½ cup (75 g/2.7 oz) firmly packed flax meal

½ cup (45 g/1.6 oz) grated Parmesan or manchego cheese

½ teaspoon salt

½ teaspoon coarse black pepper

½ teaspoon red pepper flakes

½ cup (120 ml) water

Ditch the high-carb, store-bought crackers, and whip up a batch of these thin, crispy, low-carb crackers instead! Made with nutritious seeds and flax meal plus Parmesan and a zap of red pepper flakes, they're ideal for snacking. Top them with cheese, guacamole, or my Baked Jalapeño Popper Dip (page 51).

Preheat the oven to 400°F (200°C, or gas mark 6). Place about half of the sesame seeds, pumpkin seeds, and chia seeds into a food processor and pulse a few times to break them into smaller pieces. Place in a mixing bowl and add all the remaining ingredients. Mix until well combined.

Place the dough on top of a nonstick baking mat or a piece of strong parchment paper. Place a piece of plastic wrap or parchment paper on top of the dough. Use a rolling pin to roll out the dough into a 12 ×16-inch (30 × 40-cm) rectangle. The dough should be no more than ⅛ inch (23 mm) thick. Using a pizza cutter or a large knife, precut the dough into 24 equal squares. (Precutting the dough will make the crackers easy to slice once they crisp up.)

Transfer the baking mat to a baking sheet and bake for 18 to 20 minutes. Remove from the oven. Cut or break the dough into the precut crackers. Let the crackers cool so that they become crisp. Store in an airtight container at room temperature for up to 2 weeks.

NUTRITION FACTS PER SERVING (2 CRACKERS): Total carbs: 4.4 g | Fiber: 3.4 g | Net carbs: 1 g | Protein: 4.5 g | Fat: 7.5 g | Calories: 97 kcal
MACRONUTRIENT RATIO: Calories from carbs (4%), protein (20%), fat (76%)

Baked Jalapeño Popper Dip

14 SERVINGS
HANDS-ON TIME: 10 MINUTES
OVERALL TIME: 50 MINUTES

10 slices (300 g/10.6 oz) bacon, sliced

1 large (150 g/5.3 oz) red onion, sliced

1½ cups (360 g/12.7 oz) cream cheese

¼ cup (58 g/2 oz) sour cream

½ cup (110 g/3.9 oz) Mayonnaise (page 163)

1½ cups (170 g/6 oz) shredded Cheddar cheese

1½ cups (170 g/6 oz) shredded mozzarella or Monterey Jack cheese

2 cloves garlic, minced

5 medium (70 g/2.5 oz) jalapeño peppers, sliced, or use ½ cup (70 g/2.5 oz) canned sliced jalapeño peppers

½ cup (45 g/1.6 oz) grated Parmesan cheese

Speedy Keto Crackers (page 50), Sourdough Keto Buns (page 10), or crispy veggies, for serving

None of your guests will be able to resist this keto appetizer—whether they're eating low-carb or not. It's the perfect mélange of flavors, because it features what I like to call the four major food groups: salty, crispy bacon; sweet, caramelized onions; hot jalapeños; and soft, gooey cheese. Serve it with Speedy Keto Crackers (page 50) or low-carb vegetables.

Preheat the oven to 400°F (200°C, or gas mark 6). Spread the bacon evenly on a baking tray. Transfer to the oven and bake for about 5 minutes. Then add the sliced onion and mix with the crisped-up bacon. Return to the oven and bake for 10 minutes more. Remove from the oven and place on a cooling rack. Reduce the oven temperature to 350°F (175°C, or gas mark 4).

In a deep baking dish or a casserole dish, combine the cream cheese, sour cream, mayonnaise, Cheddar, mozzarella, garlic, and jalapeños (reserving a few jalapeño slices for garnish). Add the crisped-up bacon and onion, and combine well using a large spoon. Top with the grated Parmesan, and transfer to the oven. Bake for 25 to 30 minutes, or until bubbly and golden on top.

Remove from the oven, and set aside to cool for 5 minutes. Optionally, top with more jalapeño slices. Serve with keto crackers, keto buns, or crispy veggies.

NUTRITION FACTS PER SERVING (⅓ CUP/85 G/3 OZ): Total carbs: 3.6 g | Fiber: 0.4 g | Net carbs: 3.2 g | Protein: 11.9 g | Fat: 27.2 g | Calories: 293 kcal
MACRONUTRIENT RATIO: Calories from carbs (4%), protein (16%), fat (80%)

Crispy Ranch Chicken Wings

6 SERVINGS
HANDS-ON TIME: 20 MINUTES
OVERALL TIME: 1 HOUR 30 MINUTES

CRISPY CHICKEN WINGS

18 chicken wings (about 1.5 kg/3.3 lb)

1½ tablespoons (18 g/0.6 oz) gluten-free baking powder (do not replace with baking soda)

¾ teaspoon sea salt

1½ tablespoons (23 ml) ghee or duck fat, melted

RANCH DRESSING

¼ cup (58 g/2 oz) sour cream

¼ cup (60 ml) heavy whipping cream

½ cup (110 g/3.9 oz) Mayonnaise (page 163)

2 medium (30 g/1.1 oz) spring onions, sliced

1 clove garlic, minced

2 tablespoons (8 g/0.3 oz) chopped fresh parsley or 2 teaspoons dried parsley

1 tablespoon (4 g/0.2 oz) chopped fresh dill or 1 teaspoon dried dill

1 tablespoon (15 ml) apple cider vinegar or fresh lemon juice

¼ teaspoon paprika

Sea salt and black pepper, to taste

A party isn't a party without a platter of hot, crispy chicken wings! Luckily, it's easy to make them low-carb. Serve them with my homemade ranch dressing: it's a cooling counterpart to the wings' just-out-of-the-oven crunch. Save leftovers (if there are any, that is!) for a filling keto snack the next day.

Preheat the oven to 250°F (120°C, or gas mark ½). Place the oven racks in the lower-middle and upper-middle positions in the oven. Use a baking tray deep enough to gather the fat as the chicken wings bake. Line the tray with baking foil to make it easy to clean. Place a rack on top of the foil.

TO MAKE THE CHICKEN WINGS: Use a sharp knife or meat scissors to cut the wings at the joints: you will end up with three pieces per wing. Pat all the pieces dry using a paper towel. Store the 18 wing tips in the freezer to make Bone Broth (page 160) or chicken stock. Place the remaining wing pieces (you should have 36 pieces) in a large resealable bag or a bowl. Add the baking powder and salt. Toss to coat on all sides.

Place the wings on the rack skin-side up and spread them in a single layer. Brush each piece with the ghee, then bake the wings on the lower-middle rack for 30 minutes. Then, move the wings to the upper-middle rack, increase the temperature to 425°F (220°C, or gas mark 7), and bake for another 40 to 50 minutes. Rotate the tray halfway to ensure even cooking. When done, remove the tray from the oven and let the wings rest for 5 minutes before serving.

TO MAKE THE DRESSING: While the wings are baking, mix all the ingredients in a bowl. Season with salt and pepper to taste, and serve with the crispy chicken wings.

NUTRITION FACTS PER SERVING (6 CHICKEN PIECES + 3 TABLESPOONS/45 ML RANCH DRESSING): Total carbs: 2.1 g | Fiber: 0.2 g | Net carbs: 1.9 g | Protein: 23.2 g | Fat: 44.3 g | Calories: 505 kcal
MACRONUTRIENT RATIO: Calories from carbs (2%), protein (19%), fat (79%)

CHICKEN CAESAR SALAD WITH POACHED EGG, PAGE 72

CHAPTER 4

STICK-TO-YOUR-RIBS
Soups and Hearty Salads

TOP: CREAMY "POTATO" SOUP, PAGE 65
ABOVE: STUFFED AVOCADO TWO WAYS, PAGE 73

RATATOUILLE SOUP, PAGE 64

HUNGARIAN GOULASH, PAGE 66

ABOVE LEFT: CARNE ASADA SALAD, PAGE 71
RANCH SALAD IN A JAR, PAGE 70

FOLLOWING A HEALTHY KETO DIET—WITHOUT FALLING OFF THE WAGON—can be challenging, especially during weekdays when time tends to be short. That's when it's all too easy to reach for packaged or processed foods, or to tell yourself, "Just this once!" and resort to a sugar- or carb-laden treat, kicking your body right out of ketosis.

But you can avoid traps like these when you prepare daytime meals, such as the hearty soups and salads in this chapter, in advance. Make a batch of Cheeseburger Soup (page 59); creamy, meaty, and balanced out with low-carb vegetables, it's every bit as good as it sounds. Try my low-carb Clam Chowder (page 63), which tastes just like the traditional New England version, minus the nasty white flour. Or pack up my Ranch Salad in a Jar (page 70) and bring it to work with you in the morning: it stays fresh for up to three days in the fridge, and it's super-filling (not to mention fun to eat!).

Plus, all of these recipes do double duty as light, keto-friendly dinners, so you'll have no trouble using up leftovers—if there are any, that is!

Slovak Sauerkraut Soup

10 SERVINGS
HANDS-ON TIME: 20 MINUTES
OVERALL TIME: 2 HOURS

1.3 pounds (600 g) pork shoulder

¼ cup (56 g/2 oz) ghee or lard

¼ teaspoon ground cloves

¼ teaspoon nutmeg

1.3 pounds (600 g) sauerkraut

1½ cups (45 g/1.6 oz) dried wild
    mushrooms

2 cloves garlic, crushed

2 tablespoons (30 g/1.1 oz)
    unsweetened tomato paste

1 teaspoon whole peppercorns

1 teaspoon salt

1 tablespoon (7 g/0.24 oz) caraway
    seeds

4 bay leaves

2 cups (480 ml) Bone Broth
    (page 160)

1½ quarts (1.5 L) water

1 large (200 g/7.1 oz) Hungarian
    salami

1 medium (500 g/1.1 lb) rutabaga

Optional: 1 cup (240 ml) heavy
    whipping cream

This stick-to-your-ribs soup is based on an Eastern European version that's made each winter during the holiday season. And it really is a celebration in a bowl. Tangy sauerkraut and earthy wild mushrooms bring out the best in pork, and a sprinkling of warming winter spices will make your kitchen smell like Christmas—at any time of year.

Dice the pork into medium-size pieces. Heat the ghee in a large pot and then add the pork, ground cloves, and nutmeg. Brown the meat on all sides, stirring frequently.

Add the sauerkraut, dried mushrooms, crushed garlic, tomato purée, peppercorns, salt, caraway seeds, bay leaves, bone broth, and water. Cover with a lid and let the mixture simmer for 60 to 75 minutes, or until the sauerkraut is tender.

Slice the sausage. Peel and dice the rutabaga into medium-size pieces and set aside. Once the sauerkraut is tender, add the sausage and rutabaga, and cook for another 15 to 20 minutes, or until the rutabaga is tender. If using heavy whipping cream, pour it in now and mix well. When done, remove the soup from the heat and taste. Season it with more salt if needed. Remove the peppercorns and bay leaves before serving. Try with a dollop of sour cream and a side of Sourdough Keto Buns (page 10).

NOTES:
- If you don't eat pork, you can use beef, such as braising steak, instead; however, beef may require additional cooking time.
- If you think the soup will be too sour for you, place the sauerkraut in a colander and rinse with cold water before adding it to the soup.
- Use a spice bag for easy removal of the peppercorns and bay leaf when the soup is done.

NUTRITION FACTS PER SERVING (ABOUT 2 CUPS/480 ML): Total carbs: 11.8 g | Fiber: 4 g | Net carbs: 7.7 g | Protein: 17.7 g | Fat: 25.5 g | Calories: 345 kcal
MACRONUTRIENT RATIO: Calories from carbs (9%), protein (21%), fat (70%)

Cheeseburger Soup

4 SERVINGS (ABOUT 6 CUPS/1.4 L)
HANDS-ON TIME: 15 MINUTES
OVERALL TIME: 30 MINUTES

1 small (55 g/1.9 oz) white or yellow onion, finely diced

1 clove garlic, minced

1 tablespoon (15 g/0.5 oz) ghee or lard

1 medium (200 g/7.1 oz) rutabaga

14.1 ounces (400 g) ground beef

2 cups (480 ml) Bone Broth (page 160), chicken stock, or vegetable stock

½ cup (120 g/4.2 oz) unsweetened canned tomatoes

1 medium (40 g/1.4 oz) celery stalk, sliced

½ cup (70 g/2.5 oz) sliced pickles

⅓ cup (75 g/2.6 oz) full-fat sour cream

1 cup (110 g/3.9 oz) grated Cheddar cheese, divided

1 tablespoon (4 g/0.1 oz) chopped parsley, plus more for garnish

½ cup (120 ml) heavy whipping cream

3 pastured egg yolks

Salt and pepper, to taste

Who can say no to a cheeseburger? Not me! Here, I've transformed everyone's favorite fast-food indulgence (minus the bun, of course!) into a low-carb soup that's so nourishing and comforting. Serve it with a Keto Sourdough Bun (page 10). There's no better way to beat the winter blues!

Place the onion and garlic in a large soup pot greased with the ghee. Cook over medium heat until fragrant, 3 to 5 minutes. Peel and dice the rutabaga into ½-inch (1-cm) pieces and set aside. Add the beef to the pot and cook for a few minutes, until browned on all sides. Pour in the bone broth, add the canned tomatoes, and bring to a boil. Add the rutabaga and celery, and cook for about 5 minutes over medium heat. Add the pickles and cook for another 10 minutes, or until the rutabaga is tender. Add the sour cream. Add the Cheddar cheese, reserving some for topping. Add the parsley and mix well.

Reduce the heat to medium-low. Whisk the cream with the egg yolks in a bowl. (Reserve the leftover egg whites for another use.) Slowly pour the mixture into the soup while stirring. Cook for another minute, then remove from the heat. Season with salt and pepper to taste, top with parsley and the remaining grated Cheddar, and serve.

NUTRITION FACTS PER SERVING (ABOUT 1½ CUPS/360 ML): Total carbs: 10.5 g | Fiber: 2.2 g | Net carbs: 8.3 g | Protein: 30 g | Fat: 54.6 g | Calories: 657 kcal
MACRONUTRIENT RATIO: Calories from carbs (5%), protein (19%), fat (76%)

Greek Meatball Soup

4 SERVINGS (ABOUT 5 CUPS/1.2 L +
12 MEATBALLS)
HANDS-ON TIME: 20 MINUTES
OVERALL TIME: 30 MINUTES

MEATBALLS

1 tablespoon (15 g/0.5 oz) ghee or
   lard

1½ cups (180 g/6.3 oz) uncooked
   plain Cauliflower Rice (page 13)

1.1 pounds (500 g) ground lamb or
   beef

1 large pastured egg

¼ cup (15 g/0.5 oz) chopped parsley,
   divided

2 tablespoons (8 g/0.3 oz) chopped
   dill

2 teaspoons onion powder

½ teaspoon ground coriander

½ teaspoon salt

Black pepper, to taste

AVGOLEMONO

4 cups (960 ml) beef stock or
   chicken stock

3 large pastured eggs

½ cup (120 ml) fresh lemon juice
   (2 to 3 lemons)

¼ cup (60 ml) extra-virgin olive oil

This traditional Greek soup is based on my partner Nikos's family recipe, and I love it. Best of all, it only needed a couple of tweaks to make it low-carb. It's finished with a mixture of egg, stock, and lemon juice, known as *avgolemono* in Greek; this thickens the soup and lends it a bright, citrusy flavor (not to mention a little extra protein).

TO MAKE THE MEATBALLS: Grease a pan with the ghee and cook the cauliflower rice for 5 to 7 minutes, stirring occasionally. When done, remove from the heat. Place the ground lamb and egg into a bowl. Add the parsley, reserving some for garnish. Add the dill, onion powder, coriander, salt, and pepper. Add the cooked cauliflower rice, and mix until well combined. Shape into 12 medium-size meatballs and set aside.

TO MAKE THE AVGOLEMONO: Place the stock in a saucepan and bring to a boil. Turn the heat down to medium-low. Using a slotted spoon, add the meatballs to the boiling stock. Cover with a lid and cook over medium heat for 12 to 15 minutes.

Crack the eggs into a bowl and whisk until frothy. Add the lemon juice and keep whisking. Use a ladle to slowly pour 3 to 4 ladles of the hot stock into the bowl while whisking (in order to bring the egg mix and stock to about the same temperature). Slowly pour the egg and lemon mixture back into the saucepan with the meatballs. Cook for 2 to 3 more minutes over medium heat. Remove from the heat. Just before serving, sprinkle with the reserved parsley and drizzle with the extra-virgin olive oil.

NUTRITION FACTS PER SERVING (ABOUT 1¼ CUPS/300 ML + 3 MEATBALLS): Total carbs: 6.6 g | Fiber: 1.4 g | Net carbs: 5.2 g | Protein: 32.6 g | Fat: 51.2 g | Calories: 608 kcal
MACRONUTRIENT RATIO: Calories from carbs (3%), protein (21%), fat (75%)

Clam Chowder

6 SERVINGS (ABOUT 7½ CUPS/1.8 L)
HANDS-ON TIME: 20 MINUTES
OVERALL TIME: 25 MINUTES

- 1.2 pounds (550 g) chopped clams or mussels (3 cans [6.5 oz/182 g each]) including the juice
- ½ medium (300 g/10.6 oz) head cauliflower
- 2 tablespoons (30 g/1.1 oz) ghee or butter
- 1 small (70 g/2.5 oz) white or yellow onion, finely chopped
- 2 cloves garlic, minced
- 2 medium (80 g/2.8 oz) celery stalks, sliced
- 1 cup (240 ml) additional clam juice, or chicken stock or vegetable stock
- 1 cup (240 ml) heavy whipping cream
- 1 cup (230 g/8.1 oz) sour cream
- Salt and pepper, to taste
- 2 tablespoons (8 g/0.3 oz) chopped fresh parsley, divided
- 3 large slices (48 g/1.7 oz) crispy bacon, sliced, for topping

Chowders are usually strictly verboten on a keto diet. That's because they're often jammed with potatoes, flour, and other high-carb ingredients. Not this one, though! My Clam Chowder is keto-friendly, but it's still incredibly rich, thick, and creamy—not to mention quick and easy to make. If you can't find canned clams in a store near you, try canned mussels instead; they work just as well.

Drain the clams and reserve the clam juice. Set aside. Cut the cauliflower into 1-inch (2.5-cm) florets. Heat a large soup pot or a Dutch oven greased with the ghee over medium-high heat. Add the onion and garlic. Cook until fragrant, 2 to 3 minutes. Add the celery and cauliflower, and sauté for 1 minute.

Pour in the reserved clam juice and additional clam juice or stock. Bring to a boil, then cover with a lid and reduce the heat to medium. Cook for 5 to 8 minutes, or until the cauliflower is tender. Add the cream, sour cream, and clams, mix well, and heat through for 3 to 5 minutes. Season with salt and pepper to taste. Mix in half the chopped parsley. Serve topped with the remaining parsley and the crispy bacon pieces.

NOTE:
To make the soup extra-thick, try mixing 4 to 6 egg yolks into the 1 cup (240 ml) of cream.

NUTRITION FACTS PER SERVING (ABOUT 1¼ CUPS/300 ML): Total carbs: 9.7 g | Fiber: 1.5 g | Net carbs: 8.2 g | Protein: 19.5 g | Fat: 30.4 g | Calories: 392 kcal
MACRONUTRIENT RATIO: Calories from carbs (9%), protein (20%), fat (71%)

Ratatouille Soup

6 SERVINGS
HANDS-ON TIME: 10 MINUTES
OVERALL TIME: 35 MINUTES

SOUP

2 tablespoons (30 g/1.1 oz) ghee or
  extra-virgin olive oil
1 small (110 g/3.9 oz) yellow onion,
  chopped
2 cloves garlic, minced
1 medium (120 g/4.2 oz) green
  pepper, diced
1 medium (120 g/4.2 oz) yellow or
  orange pepper, diced
1 medium (200 g/7.1 oz) zucchini,
  diced
1 medium (250 g/8.8 oz) eggplant,
  diced
1 teaspoon dried oregano
14.1 ounces (400 g) canned diced
  tomatoes
2 cups (480 ml) vegetable stock or
  chicken stock
2 cups (480 ml) water
2 tablespoons (30 g/1.1 oz) Red Pesto
  (page 168)
Salt and pepper, to taste

TOPPING

6 ounces (170 g) fresh mozzarella
  di bufala
6 tablespoons (90 ml) extra-virgin
  olive oil , for serving
Fresh basil, for garnish

Ratatouille is a vegetarian French stew that's based around naturally low-carb vegetables, like tomatoes, peppers, zucchini, and eggplant. And it's so good that I decided to turn it into a quick, no-fuss, keto soup. Drape some fresh mozzarella over each bowl just before serving, and drizzle with olive oil to add plenty of heart-healthy fats.

TO MAKE THE SOUP: Heat a skillet greased with ghee over medium heat. Add the onion and cook over medium-high heat for 5 to 8 minutes, until lightly browned. Add the garlic, peppers, zucchini, and eggplant. Cook for 1 to 2 minutes, stirring frequently. Add the oregano, tomatoes, vegetable stock, and water. Bring to a boil and cook over medium heat for about 15 minutes, or until the vegetables are tender. Remove from the heat.

Use a ladle to transfer half of the vegetables to a bowl and set aside. Use an immersion blender to purée the remaining vegetables. Place the reserved vegetables back into the pot and add the pesto. Stir and season with salt and pepper.

FOR TOPPING: To serve, ladle the soup into serving bowls and top with a piece of fresh mozzarella cheese. Drizzle each bowl with a tablespoon (15 ml) of olive oil and garnish with basil leaves. To store, let it cool, and refrigerate in an airtight container for up to 5 days or freeze for up to 3 months (without the topping).

NUTRITION FACTS PER SERVING (ABOUT 1½ CUPS/360 ML): Total carbs: 11.9 g | Fiber: 3.7 g | Net carbs: 8.2 g | Fat: 29.1 g | Calories: 338 kcal
MACRONUTRIENT RATIO: Calories from carbs (10%), protein (11%), fat (79%)

Creamy "Potato" Soup

8 SERVINGS
HANDS-ON TIME: 15 MINUTES
OVERALL TIME: 25 MINUTES

½ cup (15 g/0.5 oz) dried porcini
mushrooms

⅓ cup (73 g/2.6 oz) ghee or extra-
virgin olive oil

1 small (70 g/2.5 oz) yellow onion

2 large (128 g/4.5 oz) celery stalks,
sliced

1 small (60 g/2.1 oz) carrot, peeled
and sliced

2 cloves garlic, minced

1 small (500 g/1.1 lb) cauliflower,
chopped into florets

1 medium (400 g/14.1 oz) rutabaga,
peeled and cut into 1-inch
(2.5-cm) pieces

1 teaspoon fine sea salt, or to taste

¼ teaspoon black pepper

7 cups (1.7 L) water

2 bay leaves

2 teaspoons dried marjoram

1 teaspoon caraway seeds

2 tablespoons (8 g/0.3 oz) chopped
fresh parsley

Like the Clam Chowder on page 63, this traditionally starchy soup—a family recipe—has had the unhealthy carbs edited right out of it. It's still smooth and creamy, but it replaces the potato with low-starch rutabaga and cauliflower. Serve it with Sourdough Keto Buns (page 10) or Speedy Keto Crackers (page 50).

Place the mushrooms in a cup filled with a cup (240 ml) of water and soak for 30 minutes. In a large heavy-based pot or casserole dish greased with ghee, cook the onion over medium-high heat for 5 to 8 minutes, until lightly browned. Add the celery, carrot, and garlic, and cook for another minute. Add the cauliflower, rutabaga, soaked mushrooms (including the water), salt, pepper, water, bay leaves, marjoram, and caraway seeds. Bring to a boil, and then reduce the heat to medium-low and cook, covered, for about 20 minutes.

Remove from the heat and let it cool for 10 to 15 minutes. Discard the bay leaves, then ladle half of the vegetables into a bowl and set aside. Use an immersion blender and process the remaining vegetables and stock until smooth. Add back the reserved vegetables and parsley. Season to taste and eat immediately, or let it cool and refrigerate in an airtight container for up to 5 days, or freeze for up to 3 months.

NUTRITION FACTS PER SERVING (ABOUT 1½ CUPS/360 ML): Total carbs: 11.3 g | Fiber: 3.5 g | Net carbs: 7.9 g | Protein: 2.3 g | Fat: 9.6 g | Calories: 135 kcal
MACRONUTRIENT RATIO: Calories from carbs (25%), protein (7%), fat (68%)

Hungarian Goulash

8 SERVINGS
HANDS-ON TIME: 20 MINUTES
OVERALL TIME: 2 HOURS 20 MINUTES

3 tablespoons (45 g/1.6 oz) ghee,
   duck fat, or lard
1 large (150 g/5.3 oz) yellow onion,
   chopped
2 cloves garlic, minced
2 pounds (900 g) beef chuck steak,
   cut into 1½-inch (4-cm) chunks
1 teaspoon fine sea salt, or to taste
½ teaspoon black pepper
½ teaspoon caraway seeds
½ cup (55 g/1.9 oz) paprika, divided
¼ cup (63 g/2.2 oz) unsweetened
   tomato paste
2 bay leaves
10 cups (2.4 L) water, divided
1 medium (300 g/10.6 oz) rutabaga,
   peeled and cut into 1-inch
   (2.5-cm) pieces
2 medium (240 g/8.5 oz) green bell
   peppers, sliced
6 egg yolks
2 tablespoons (8 g/0.3 oz) chopped
   fresh parsley, plus more for
   garnish
Optional: Sourdough Keto Buns
   (page 10)

This one's a serious crowd-pleaser. Goulash is an Eastern European favorite, and with good reason: it's rich, creamy, and so easy to make. Traditionally, it's ladled over hot noodles—but not in this keto version. Here, egg yolks lend the goulash its characteristic texture, and low-carb veggies, like rutabaga and peppers, make it into a healthy, balanced meal.

In a large heavy-based saucepan or a Dutch oven greased with ghee, cook the onion over medium-high heat for 5 to 8 minutes, until lightly browned. Add the garlic and beef, and cook over medium-high heat until browned on all sides. Reduce the heat to medium and add the salt, pepper, caraway seeds, and 2 tablespoons (14 g/0.5 oz) of the paprika. Add the tomato paste, bay leaves, and 9 cups (2.1 L) of the water. Reduce the heat to low, cover with a lid, and cook for about 90 minutes.

After 90 minutes, add the rutabaga and cook, covered, for another 20 minutes. Add the peppers, and cook for 5 minutes, or until the rutabaga is tender. Add the remaining 6 tablespoons (41 g/1.4 oz) paprika to the pot.

Whisk the remaining 1 cup (240 ml) water with the egg yolks. Slowly drizzle in the egg and water, and cook while stirring until it thickens. Remove from the heat and let it sit for 5 minutes before serving, garnished with parsley. Goulash pairs perfectly with Sourdough Keto Buns! To store, let it cool, and refrigerate in an airtight container for up to 4 days or freeze for up to 3 months.

NUTRITION FACTS PER SERVING (ABOUT 1½ CUPS/360 ML): Total carbs: 11.5 g | Fiber: 4.4 g | Net carbs: 7.1 g | Protein: 25.7 g | Fat: 30.3 g | Calories: 418 kcal
MACRONUTRIENT RATIO: Calories from carbs (7%), protein (25%), fat (68%)

Salmon Niçoise Salad

2 SERVINGS
HANDS-ON TIME: 15 MINUTES
OVERALL TIME: 25 MINUTES

SALAD

1½ cups (150 g/5.3 oz) raw green
   beans, trimmed
1 tablespoon (15 g/0.5 oz) ghee or
   virgin coconut oil
2 medium (250 g/8.8 oz) salmon
   fillets
Salt and pepper, to taste
2 large eggs
4 cups (120 g/4.2 oz) mixed salad
   greens
2 small (80 g/2.8 oz) tomatoes,
   sliced
½ medium (100 g/3.5 oz) cucumber,
   sliced
½ medium (40 g/1.4 oz) red onion,
   sliced
8 pitted olives (24 g/0.8 oz)
4 canned (16 g/0.6 oz) anchovies,
   chopped, or 2 tablespoons
   (17 g/0.6 oz) capers

DRESSING

3 tablespoons (45 ml) extra-virgin
   olive oil
1 tablespoon (15 ml) fresh lemon
   juice
1 clove garlic, crushed
½ teaspoon Dijon mustard
Pinch salt and pepper

Niçoise salad is a French bistro classic, and it's so easy to make it keto-friendly: all you need to do is omit the potatoes. You could use fresh tuna here, too, but I prefer salmon: as an oily fish, it's got plenty of omega-3 fatty acids. And the simple Dijon vinaigrette is so good you'll want to drizzle it on just about everything!

TO MAKE THE SALAD: Fill a saucepan with salted water and bring to a boil. Add the green beans and cook for 2 to 4 minutes, until they are just al dente. Using a slotted spoon, plunge them into a bowl of ice water to stop the cooking. Transfer them to paper towels to dry.

Grease a pan with the ghee and place over medium-high heat. Pat the salmon fillets dry with paper towels, and season with salt and pepper. Place the salmon, skin-side down, on the hot pan, and lower the heat to medium. Cook for 3 to 4 minutes per side, until the fish is firm and cooked through. (Do not force the fish out of the pan. If you try to flip the fillet and it doesn't release, give it a few more seconds until it becomes crisp, then try again.) Set the cooked fish aside.

To hard-boil the eggs, follow the instructions on page 23: For a soft-set egg yolk, leave covered for 8 to 9 minutes; for a hard-boiled one, up to 13 minutes. When done, peel and cut the eggs into quarters.

TO MAKE THE DRESSING: Combine all the ingredients in a small bowl.

To assemble the salad, place the salad greens into serving bowls. Add the tomatoes, cucumber, onion, and cooked green beans. Top with the salmon fillets (with or without the skin), quartered eggs, olives, and anchovies. Drizzle with the prepared dressing and serve.

NUTRITION FACTS PER SERVING: Total carbs: 12.5 g | Fiber: 4.3 g | Net carbs: 8.2 g | Protein: 39.1 g | Fat: 44.4 g | Calories: 605 kcal
MACRONUTRIENT RATIO: Calories from carbs (6%), protein (26%), fat (68%)

Ranch Salad in a Jar

2 SERVINGS
HANDS-ON TIME: 10 MINUTES
OVERALL TIME: 10 MINUTES

DRESSING

¼ cup (55 g/1.9 oz) Mayonnaise
  (page 163)
¼ cup (58 g/2 oz) sour cream
1 tablespoon (15 ml) apple cider
  vinegar or fresh lemon juice
¼ teaspoon onion powder
¼ teaspoon garlic powder
⅛ teaspoon paprika
1 to 2 tablespoons (4 to 8 g/0.1 to
  0.3 oz) chopped dill
Salt and pepper, to taste

SALAD

2 medium (80 g/2.8 oz) celery stalks,
  sliced
4 large eggs, hard-boiled (see page
  23), quartered
4 large (64 g/2.3 oz) slices cooked
  bacon, chopped
4 cups (120 g/4.2 oz) mixed salad
  greens

Packing salads in jars may seem like a hipster trend, but it's actually an incredibly handy technique, especially if you need to prepare a healthy keto meal in advance. Made with homemade ranch dressing, this crunchy, protein-packed Ranch Salad will stay fresh for several days in the fridge. That means you've got lunchtime all taken care of!

TO MAKE THE DRESSING: Combine the mayonnaise, sour cream, vinegar, onion powder, garlic powder, paprika, dill, salt, and pepper in a bowl. Whisk to blend well. Place the dressing at the bottom of two 1-quart (950-ml) jars with wide mouths.

  TO ASSEMBLE THE SALAD: Add a layer of celery to each jar, followed by a layer of the quartered eggs, then the bacon pieces and salad greens. When ready to serve, tip the salad over into a serving bowl so that the dressing covers the greens. Or, simply shake the jar—keeping the lid closed—and then eat the salad right from the jar. Store sealed in the fridge for up to 3 days.

NOTE:

When you're making salads in jars, be sure to put the dressing at the bottom, followed by a layer of sturdy low-carb vegetables, such as celery, cucumber, or peppers. Add a layer of protein, like eggs or meat. Finally, top with leafy greens. This style of layering will prevent the tender greens from wilting, and they'll stay fresh for longer. Use a wide-mouth jar for easy assembly—and to make it easy to decant the salad into a bowl.

NUTRITION FACTS PER SERVING: Total carbs: 5.1 g | Fiber: 1.5 g | Net carbs: 3.6 g | Protein: 24.3 g | Fat: 41.4 g | Calories: 489 kcal
MACRONUTRIENT RATIO: Calories from carbs (3%), protein (20%), fat (77%)

Carne Asada Salad

2 SERVINGS
HANDS-ON TIME: 10 MINUTES
OVERALL TIME: 15 MINUTES

SPICY CILANTRO-LIME VINAIGRETTE

1 small bunch (15 g/0.5 oz) fresh
   cilantro
1 medium (14 g/0.5 oz) jalapeño
   pepper
4 cloves garlic, chopped
½ teaspoon ground cumin
½ cup (120 ml) extra-virgin olive oil
¼ cup (60 ml) fresh lime juice
Sea salt and black pepper, to taste

SALAD

1 large (300 g/10.6 oz) flank steak or
   skirt steak
Sea salt and black pepper, to taste
1 tablespoon (15 g/0.5) ghee, lard, or
   coconut oil
1 head (200 g/7.1 oz) soft green
   lettuce, such as butterhead
   lettuce, or other leafy greens
1 medium (150 g/5.3 oz) avocado,
   pitted, peeled, and diced
1 medium (100 g/3.5 oz) tomato,
   diced
Lime wedges and fresh cilantro,
   for serving
Optional toppings: Shredded
   Cheddar cheese and sour cream

Carne asada simply means "grilled meat" in Spanish, and steak certainly does take center stage in this simple salad of meat, greens, tomato, and avocado. Don't think for a minute that "simple" equals "boring," though: the citrusy, cilantro-y vinaigrette that accompanies it is anything but! Add some cheese and sour cream before serving to make it even more filling.

TO MAKE THE VINAIGRETTE: Place all the ingredients in a blender and process until smooth. Reserve ¼ cup (60 ml) for the salad. Store any leftover dressing in the fridge for up to a week.

TO MAKE THE SALAD: Pat dry the steak and season with salt and pepper. Set a large pan greased with the ghee over high heat. Once hot, cook the steak for 3 minutes on each side (flank steak), or 2 to 3 minutes on each side (skirt steak), depending on the thickness of the meat, until medium-rare. Do not overcook the steak. Remove from the pan and keep warm.

When ready to serve, slice the meat thinly against the grain. Place the lettuce leaves in a bowl, and top with the sliced steak, avocado, and tomato. Drizzle the vinaigrette (2 tablespoons/30 ml per serving) over the salad. Serve with lime wedges and cilantro, and, optionally, with cheese and sour cream. The cooked steak can be refrigerated for up to 3 days. The dressing can be refrigerated for up to 1 week in an airtight container. Always prepare the salad right before serving.

NUTRITION FACTS PER SERVING: Total carbs: 14 g | Fiber: 7.3 g | Net carbs: 6.7 g | Protein: 35.5 g | Fat: 56.6 g | Calories: 694 kcal
MACRONUTRIENT RATIO: Calories from carbs (4%), protein (21%), fat (75%)

Chicken Caesar Salad with Poached Egg

2 SERVINGS
HANDS-ON TIME: 30 MINUTES
OVERALL TIME: 30 MINUTES

MCT SALAD DRESSING

¼ cup (55 g/1.9 oz) Mayonnaise (page 163)

1 tablespoon (15 g/0.5 oz) Dijon mustard

¼ cup (60 ml) extra-virgin olive oil

2 tablespoons (30 ml) MCT oil

2 tablespoons (30 ml) fresh lemon juice

2 cloves garlic, minced

2 tablespoons (8 g/0.3 oz) chopped herbs of your choice

Sea salt and black pepper, to taste

Optional: 4 anchovies (16 g/0.6 oz) and 1 tablespoon (5 g/0.2 oz) grated Parmesan cheese

SALAD

2 large (200 g/7.1 oz) skin-on chicken thighs, bone removed

Sea salt and black pepper, to taste

1 tablespoon (14 g/0.5 oz) duck fat or ghee

7.1 ounces (200 g) soft green lettuce, such as butterhead, or iceberg lettuce

2 large eggs, poached (see page 23)

2 slices (32 g/1.1 oz) cooked bacon

2 ounces (57 g) shaved Parmesan cheese

This hearty chicken Caesar makes a satisfying lunch (or dinner, for that matter). It's full of protein, of course, and its dressing offers extra benefits in the form of MCT oil. "MCT" stands for medium-chain triglycerides, and it's a type of fat that may promote healthy brain function and weight loss. To make your own low-carb croutons, just toast and then dice a Sourdough Keto Bun (page 10).

TO MAKE THE DRESSING: Process all the ingredients in a blender. Reserve ¼ cup (60 ml) for the salad. Any leftover salad dressing can be stored in the fridge for up to 5 days.

TO MAKE THE SALAD: Pat the chicken thighs dry with a paper towel, and season them with salt and pepper on both sides. Grease a skillet with the duck fat and heat over high heat. Place the chicken thighs, skin-side down, into the hot pan. Cook for about 2 minutes, then reduce the heat to medium and cook for another 3 minutes, or until the skin is golden brown. Flip the chicken thighs over and cook for about 5 minutes more. The thighs are done when a thermometer inserted into the thickest part of the thigh reads at least 165°F (74°C). When done, transfer to a plate. Set aside for 5 minutes, then slice into thin strips.

To assemble the salad, tear the lettuce into pieces and divide between 2 bowls. Add the sliced chicken, poached egg, bacon, Parmesan, and Sourdough Keto Bun croutons, if using (see headnote). Drizzle with the prepared dressing. Eat immediately. To store, keep the ingredients in separate containers in the fridge. Reheat the chicken and the poached egg and assemble before serving.

NUTRITION FACTS PER SERVING: Total carbs: 5.1 g | Fiber: 1.5 g | Net carbs: 3.6 g | Protein: 37 g | Fat: 63.8 g | Calories: 742 kcal
MACRONUTRIENT RATIO: Calories from carbs (2%), protein (20%), fat (78%)

Stuffed Avocados Two Ways

4 SERVINGS
HANDS-ON TIME: 15 MINUTES
OVERALL TIME: 15 MINUTES

CHICKEN PESTO–STUFFED AVOCADO

2 medium (240 g/8.5 oz) cooked
    chicken breasts, diced

2 tablespoons (30 g/1.1 oz) Basil Pesto
    (page 167)

2 tablespoons (30 g/1.1 oz) Mayonnaise
    (page 163)

1 tablespoon (15 ml) fresh lemon juice

8 large (50 g/1.8 oz) pitted green olives

3 pieces (20 g/0.7 oz) sun-dried
    tomatoes, chopped

Salt and pepper, to taste

GREEK SALAD–STUFFED AVOCADO

½ medium (60 g/2.1 oz) green pepper,
    sliced

½ small (30 g/1.1 oz) red onion, sliced

1 small (150 g/5.3 oz) cucumber, peeled
    and diced

3 medium (150 g/5.3 oz) tomatoes,
    chopped

⅔ cup (100 g/3.5 oz) crumbled feta

16 pitted (25 g/0.9 oz) olives,
    preferably kalamata, sliced

1 teaspoon dried oregano

4 tablespoons (60 ml) extra-virgin
    olive oil

2 extra-large or 4 medium
    (600 g/1.3 lbs) avocados

Fresh basil, for garnish

Black pepper, for garnish

I'm obsessed with stuffed avocados: they're just so versatile! You can fill them with the Chicken Pesto or Greek Salad options below, or pack them with Avocado-Egg Salad (page 47, Avocado-Egg Stuffed Bacon Cups). Or, use pulled pork, canned tuna, or canned salmon as the main ingredient in your own custom-made filling. The options are endless!

TO MAKE THE CHICKEN PESTO–STUFFED AVOCADOS: Place the chicken in a mixing bowl. Add the pesto, mayonnaise, and lemon juice. Add the olives and sun-dried tomatoes. Season with salt and pepper to taste. Optionally, cover with plastic wrap and place in the fridge to marinate for 2 hours or overnight.

TO MAKE THE GREEK SALAD–STUFFED AVOCADOS: Place all the vegetables in a bowl and add the feta, olives, and oregano. Drizzle with the olive oil and set aside.

Leaving a ½-inch (1-cm) layer of avocado along the insides of the skins, scoop the middle of the avocado halves out, cut into small pieces, and add to the bowl with either the marinated chicken or the Greek salad. Combine well and fill the avocado halves with the mixture. Garnish with the fresh basil and black pepper, and serve immediately.

NUTRITION FACTS PER SERVING (½ LARGE CHICKEN PESTO AVOCADO/GREEK SALAD AVOCADO): Total carbs: 15.2/18 g | Fiber: 11/11.6 g | Net carbs: 4.2/6.4 g | Protein: 21.1/7.5 g | Fat: 37.5/42.6 g | Calories: 462/460 kcal
MACRONUTRIENT RATIO: Calories from carbs (4/6%), protein (19/7%), fat (77/87%)

EGGPLANT PARMA HAM ROLLS, PAGE 78

TACO FRITTATA, PAGE 79

CHAPTER 5

EASY, LOW-STARCH
Lunches

BACON-WRAPPED BEEF PATTIES WITH
CHIMIOLE, PAGE 82

MEXICAN CHICKEN BOWLS, PAGE 85

SPICED COCONUT
GRANOLA BARS, PAGE 89

TURKEY NUGGETS WITH KALE SLAW & ITALIAN DRESSING, PAGE 84

HAM & CHEESE BREAD ROLLS, PAGE 86

ARE YOU CONSTANTLY STARVING BY THE TIME
noon rolls around, even if you've had a healthy breakfast?
If so, join the club! I always seem to be hungry around
midday, which is why this chapter includes a whole host
of lunchtime recipes that'll keep you energized and sated
until dinnertime.

If you have a little extra time on your hands, make the
Vegetable Rose Pie on page 77. It features keto-friendly
vegetable ribbons wound into rosettes and stuffed into a
savory crust: its presentation is nothing short of stunning,
and you won't believe it's low-carb. Lunch (or brunch)
guests will love the Taco Frittata on page 79, which crams
all the best parts of a taco—*sans* high-carb shells—into one
high-protein, single-skillet dish.

But if it's a workday and time is of the essence, pop
some portable Eggplant Parma Ham Rolls (page 78) or
Ham & Cheese Bread Rolls (page 86) into your lunchbox
along with some raw low-carb veggies. Or, stick a couple
of grain-free Spiced Coconut Granola Bars (page 89) into
your bag. They're a great stand-in for lunch when you're on
the go: no kitchen required.

Vegetable Rose Pie

12 SERVINGS
HANDS-ON TIME: 30 MINUTES
OVERALL TIME: 1 HOUR 30 MINUTES

This keto "rose" pie features colorful, low-carb vegetable ribbons, a grain-free crust, and lots of cheese to help you stay sated.

CRUST

1½ cups (150 g/5.3 oz) almond flour

1 cup (90 g/3.2 oz) grated Parmesan cheese, or other hard cheese

1 large egg

2 tablespoons (30 g/1.1 oz) butter

FILLING

3 medium (600 g/1.3 lb) zucchini (use green and yellow for a "rainbow" effect)

1 large (400 g/14.1 oz) eggplant

1 tablespoon (15 ml) fresh lemon juice

1 tablespoon (15 ml) melted ghee

Sea salt and black pepper

1 cup (240 g/8.5 oz) mascarpone cheese

½ cup (125 g/4.4 oz) Basil Pesto (page 167)

1 cup (120 g/4.2 oz) grated Swiss cheese

⅓ cup (30 g/1.1 oz) grated Parmesan cheese

2 large eggs

1 tablespoon (15 ml) extra-virgin olive oil

Fresh basil or thyme, for garnish

TO MAKE THE CRUST: Preheat the oven to 350°F (175°C, or gas mark 4). Place all the ingredients for the crust in a bowl, and mix until well combined. Press into a pie pan toward the edges to create a bowl shape so that the pie can hold the filling. The edges should be at least 1¼ inches (3 cm) tall. Bake for 10 to 12 minutes, or until golden brown.

TO MAKE THE FILLING: Slice the zucchini into long, thin ribbons. Do the same for the eggplant, then halve the ribbons lengthwise to create thinner ribbons. Lay the zucchini and eggplant ribbons on baking trays lined with parchment paper. Drizzle with the lemon juice and brush with the melted ghee. Season with salt and pepper. When the crust is ready, remove from the oven and cool on a rack. Increase the temperature to 400°F (200°C, or gas mark 6), and bake the ribbons for 15 to 18 minutes, until soft. Remove from the oven and let them cool down for a few minutes.

Place the mascarpone, pesto, Swiss cheese, Parmesan, eggs, and salt and pepper to taste into a bowl, and mix until well combined. Spoon the filling into the prepared crust.

Reduce the temperature to 300°F (150°C). Stack 2 slices of zucchini and eggplant on top of each other. Starting from one end, roll the stack into a spiral and press it into the filling so that it stands up in the center of the pie. Create a layer from another three vegetable slices and wrap these stacks around the spiral in the center. Repeat until the pie is complete: you will have created a rose effect and very little of the filling will be visible.

Bake for 35 to 40 minutes, until set. Remove from the oven and let it cool for 15 minutes. Drizzle with the olive oil and garnish with fresh herbs. Serve warm or cold. Store refrigerated for up to 5 days.

NUTRITION FACTS PER SERVING (1 SLICE): Total carbs: 7.4 g | Fiber: 3 g | Net carbs: 4.4 g | Protein: 13.3 g | Fat: 32 g | Calories: 361 kcal
MACRONUTRIENT RATIO: Calories from carbs (5%), protein (15%), fat (80%)

Eggplant Parma Ham Rolls

3 SERVINGS (6 ROLLS)
HANDS-ON TIME: 15 MINUTES
OVERALL TIME: 30 MINUTES

EGGPLANT

1 medium (250 g/8.8 oz) eggplant

2 tablespoons (30 g/1.1 oz) ghee,
   melted, or extra-virgin olive oil

¼ teaspoon salt, or to taste

Pepper

FILLING

5.3 oz (150 g) soft goat cheese

2 tablespoons (30 g/1.1 oz) Basil
   Pesto (page 167) or Red Pesto
   (page 168)

LEMON VINAIGRETTE

2 tablespoons (30 ml) extra-virgin
   olive oil

1 tablespoon (15 ml) fresh lemon
   juice

1 teaspoon balsamic vinegar

FOR SERVING

6 slices (85 g/3 oz) Parma ham

6 cups (180 g/6.3 oz) fresh spinach
   or other leafy greens

Fresh basil

Black pepper

Make these eggplant (or aubergine) rolls ahead of time, then pop them into your lunchbox or keep a plate of them in the fridge for a simple keto lunch; just pair them with a green salad. In addition to being naturally low-carb, eggplant has a host of potential health benefits: the phytochemicals in its dark purple skin may promote heart health and improve blood flow to the brain.

TO MAKE THE EGGPLANT: Preheat the oven to 400°F (200°C, or gas mark 6). Cut the eggplant lengthwise into 6 slices about ½ inch (1 cm) each. Place on a baking sheet lined with parchment paper. Brush the eggplant on both sides with melted ghee. Season with salt and pepper. Transfer to the oven and bake for 15 to 18 minutes, until cooked through. Set aside to cool.

MEANWHILE, TO MAKE THE FILLING: Place the goat cheese and pesto in a bowl. Mix until well combined.

TO MAKE THE VINAIGRETTE: In another bowl, combine the olive oil, lemon juice, and balsamic vinegar.

TO ASSEMBLE THE ROLLS: Place a slice of Parma ham onto each slice of the eggplant, spread with about 2 tablespoons of the goat cheese filling, and roll them up. Serve on a bed of spinach (2 cups [60 g/2.1 oz] per serving). Drizzle with the lemon vinaigrette, and garnish with basil leaves and black pepper. Serve immediately, or store the eggplant rolls (without spinach) in an airtight container in the fridge for up to 3 days.

NUTRITION FACTS PER SERVING (2 ROLLS + GREENS): Total carbs: 8.6 g | Fiber: 4.1 g | Net carbs: 4.5 g | Protein: 19.5 g | Fat: 39.8 g | Calories: 462 kcal
MACRONUTRIENT RATIO: Calories from carbs (4%), protein (17%), fat (79%)

Taco Frittata

3 SERVINGS (6 SLICES)
HANDS-ON TIME: 20 MINUTES
OVERALL TIME: 30 MINUTES

2 tablespoons (30 g/1.1 oz) ghee or
  lard
1 small (70 g/2.5 oz) white onion,
  chopped
½ medium (125 g/4.4 oz) eggplant
8.8 ounces (250 g) ground beef
1 tablespoon (8 g/0.3 oz) taco
  seasoning
2 tablespoons (30 ml) water
6 large eggs
½ cup (60 g/2.1 oz) grated Cheddar
  cheese
¼ cup (25 g/0.9 oz) sliced black
  olives

Frittatas aren't just for breakfast or brunch: they also make fabulous light lunches or dinners. This taco-inspired version is a perfect example. Loaded with meat, cheese, olives, and taco seasoning—and low-carb eggplant in place of beans—it's full of good-quality protein. Top with sour cream, avocado, and salsa for an even more substantial meal.

Heat a large pan greased with ghee over medium heat. Add the onion and cook until fragrant, about 3 minutes. Meanwhile, dice the eggplant into ½-inch (1-cm) pieces. Add to the pan and cook for another 5 minutes. Add the ground beef, taco seasoning, and water, and cook for 3 to 5 minutes, until the meat is browned on all sides and the eggplant is tender.

Preheat the broiler. Crack the eggs into a bowl and whisk with a fork. Add the Cheddar cheese and sliced olives to the pan, then pour in the whisked eggs. Stir to combine and cook until firm, about 10 minutes. Finally, place the pan under the broiler and cook for 5 minutes to crisp up the top.

Let the frittata cool slightly and cut it into 6 pieces. Once completely cooled, store in the fridge in an airtight container for up to 5 days.

NUTRITION FACTS PER SERVING (⅓ FRITTATA, 2 SLICES): Total carbs: 6.9 g | Fiber: 2.5 g | Net carbs: 4.4 g | Protein: 32.7 g | Fat: 45 g | Calories: 569 kcal
MACRONUTRIENT RATIO: Calories from carbs (3%), protein (24%), fat (73%)

Greek Zucchini and Feta Fritters

3 SERVINGS (9 PATTIES)
HANDS-ON TIME: 15 MINUTES
OVERALL TIME: 25 MINUTES

2 medium (400 g/14.1 oz) zucchini
½ teaspoon salt, or more to taste
½ cup (45 g/1.6 oz) grated Parmesan cheese or hard cheese of choice
2 large pastured eggs
1 teaspoon ground cumin
½ cup (75 g/2.6 oz) crumbled feta cheese
¼ cup (25 g/0.9 oz) sliced olives
2 tablespoons (8 g/0.3 oz) chopped mixed herbs (such as mint, oregano, and dill)
2 tablespoons (30 g/1.1 oz) ghee or lard

Laced with Mediterranean herbs, spices, and olives, these cheesy vegetarian fritters make an ideal lunch on warm summer days when you just don't feel like eating meat. And when unexpected guests turn up, they work well as appetizers, too. Dip them in sour cream, Greek yogurt, or guacamole—or even all three.

Use a julienne peeler or a spiralizer to create thin "noodles" from the zucchini. Sprinkle them with salt and let sit for 10 minutes. Use a paper towel to pat them dry. (If any noodles are very long, cut them in half.)

Place the zucchini, Parmesan cheese, eggs, cumin, feta, olives, and herbs in a bowl. Combine well. Create 9 small patties from the mixture and fry them in a hot pan greased with the ghee, about 2 to 3 minutes per side. (Do not flip them too early or the patties will break.) Alternatively, you can drizzle the patties with melted ghee and bake them in an oven preheated to 400°F (200°C, or gas mark 6) for 15 to 20 minutes.

Once cooked, serve immediately with full-fat yogurt or as a side with meat, or let them cool completely and store in the fridge in an airtight container for up to 3 days.

NUTRITION FACTS PER SERVING (3 FRITTERS): Total carbs: 7.3 g | Fiber: 2.1 g | Net carbs: 5.2 g | Protein: 15 g | Fat: 25.1 g | Calories: 313 kcal
MACRONUTRIENT RATIO: Calories from carbs (7%), protein (19%), fat (74%)

Zucchini Lasagna

4 SERVINGS
HANDS-ON TIME: 10 MINUTES
OVERALL TIME: 35 TO 40 MINUTES

2 tablespoons (30 g/1.1 oz) ghee

2 cloves garlic, crushed

1.3 pounds (600 g) ground lamb

2 teaspoons dried oregano

2 teaspoons dried basil

1 tablespoon (7 g/0.25 oz) paprika

½ teaspoon salt

1 cup (240 g/8.5 oz) canned diced tomatoes

4 medium (800 g/1.7 lb) zucchini

⅔ cup (60 g/2.1 oz) grated Parmesan cheese

What do you get when you combine Italian lasagna and Greek moussaka? A low-carb zucchini-lamb lasagna that's far healthier than the original version, but just as filling. And if you ask me, it tastes even better the next day, so go ahead and make it in advance, then enjoy it for lunch all week.

Heat a large pan greased with ghee over medium heat and add the crushed garlic. Cook for 1 minute and then add the ground lamb, dried oregano, basil, paprika, and salt. Mix and cook until the meat is browned on all sides. Add the tomatoes and cook for 2 to 3 minutes. Remove from the heat and set aside.

Preheat the oven to 400°F (200°C, or gas mark 6). Meanwhile, prepare the zucchini. Wash the zucchini and use a potato peeler or a sharp knife to thinly slice the zucchini into wide "noodles."

Lay a third of the zucchini slices in a large casserole dish and top with half of the meat mixture. Add a third of the Parmesan cheese, then another layer of zucchini slices. Add the remaining layer of the meat mixture and top with more Parmesan and the last layer of the zucchini slices. Sprinkle the top of the lasagna with the remaining Parmesan cheese and place in the oven.

Cook for 25 to 30 minutes, until tender. When done, remove from the oven and set aside to cool for 10 minutes. Enjoy immediately or refrigerate when completely cool and store for up to 3 days.

NUTRITION FACTS PER SERVING: Total carbs: 11.3 g | Fiber: 3.8 g | Net carbs: 7.5 g | Protein: 34.5 g | Fat: 43.4 g | Calories: 563 kcal
MACRONUTRIENT RATIO: Calories from carbs (5%), protein (25%), fat (70%)

Bacon-Wrapped Beef Patties with "Chimiole"

4 SERVINGS
HANDS-ON TIME: 20 MINUTES
OVERALL TIME: 40 MINUTES

PATTIES

1 pound (450 g) ground beef
¼ teaspoon black pepper
½ small (35 g/1.2 oz) yellow onion, finely chopped
1 clove garlic, crushed
16 slices (240 g/8.5 oz) thin-cut bacon (about 15 g/0.5 oz per slice)

"CHIMIOLE"

2 large (400 g/14.1) avocados, pitted and peeled
1 small (70 g/2.5 oz) yellow onion, finely chopped
1⅓ cups (200 g/7.1 oz) chopped regular or cherry tomatoes
½ cup (120 ml) Chimichurri (page 171)
Sea salt and black pepper
Optional: Lettuce and freshly chopped vegetables, such as tomatoes, bell peppers, or cucumber, for serving

"Chimiole" is my very own creation: guacamole mixed with chimichurri sauce, which is a spicy, cilantro-based sauce that only takes a few seconds to whip up (see page 171). Chimiole is a big favorite in our house, and it's so delicious I could practically eat it with a spoon, but it's an especially good match for meaty, bacon-wrapped burgers.

TO MAKE THE PATTIES: Preheat the oven to 400°F (200°C, or gas mark 6). Combine the beef, pepper, onion, and garlic in a bowl. Using your hands, form the mixture into 8 medium patties (about 60 g/2.1 oz each). Wrap each of the patties with 2 slices of bacon. Place on a baking tray lined with parchment paper. Bake for 25 to 30 minutes, or until the patties are golden brown.

TO MAKE THE "CHIMIOLE": Place 1 avocado into a bowl and mash well with a fork. Add the onion, tomatoes, and chimichurri. Stir to combine. Dice the second avocado and mix it into the chimiole, but do not mash it. Season with salt and black pepper to taste.

Serve 2 patties with about 1 cup/240 g of the chimiole. Optionally, serve with lettuce and vegetables. To store, place the patties and chimiole in separate airtight containers, and store in the fridge for up to 3 days.

NUTRITION FACTS PER SERVING (2 PATTIES + 1 CUP/200 G/7 OZ "CHIMIOLE"): Total carbs: 14.9 g | Fiber: 8.8 g | Net carbs: 6.1 g | Protein: 30.5 g | Fat: 66.3 g | Calories: 768 kcal
MACRONUTRIENT RATIO: Calories from carbs (3%), protein (16%), fat (81%)

Turkey Nuggets with Kale Slaw & Italian Dressing

4 SERVINGS
HANDS-ON TIME: 10 MINUTES
OVERALL TIME: 20 MINUTES

This superfood slaw features three kinds of greens—kale, cabbage, and broccoli stalks—and lashings of fresh herbs, and they all stand up beautifully to a creamy, tomato-tinged Italian dressing. You could easily devour it on its own (I have!), but it's best served alongside easy-to-make turkey nuggets for an incredibly healthy, fiber-rich lunch.

ITALIAN DRESSING

½ cup (110 g/3.9 oz) Mayonnaise (page 163)
¼ cup (58 g/2 oz) sour cream
1 tablespoon (15 g/0.5 oz) unsweetened tomato paste
4 pieces (12 g/0.4 oz) sun-dried tomatoes, chopped
2 tablespoons (8 g/0.3 oz) chopped fresh herbs, such as parsley, basil, or thyme
Sea salt and black pepper

SUPERFOOD KALE SLAW

7.1 ounces (200 g) green cabbage
3.5 ounces (100 g) dark-leaf kale or baby kale
3 or 4 (100 g/3.5 oz) broccoli stalks, peeled, or 1 small kohlrabi
1 small (70 g/2.5 oz) red onion, sliced
2 tablespoons (30 ml) fresh lemon juice
½ teaspoon celery seeds
2 tablespoons (8 g/0.3 oz) chopped fresh herbs, such as parsley, basil, or thyme
Sea salt and black pepper

TURKEY NUGGETS

1.3 pounds (600 g) dark turkey meat
1 large egg, beaten
Pinch sea salt and black pepper
1½ cups (135 g/4.8 oz) finely grated Parmesan cheese
2 tablespoons (30 g/1.1 oz) ghee or duck fat

TO MAKE THE DRESSING: Combine all the ingredients in a small bowl. Set aside.

TO MAKE THE SLAW: Using your food processor's slicing blade, thinly slice the cabbage, kale, and broccoli stalks (or kohlrabi), then place in a large mixing bowl. Add the red onion, lemon juice, celery seeds, and herbs. Add half of the prepared dressing and combine well. Season with salt and pepper to taste, and mix well again.

TO MAKE THE TURKEY NUGGETS: Slice the turkey into 16 pieces about ½ inch (1 cm) thick. In a bowl, beat the egg with a pinch of salt and pepper. Place the Parmesan in a separate bowl. Dip each of the turkey pieces in the egg, then dip into the bowl with the Parmesan and roll to coat well. Heat a pan greased with the ghee over medium-high heat. Once hot, add the turkey nuggets, and fry until golden brown on both sides. Work in batches: do not overfill the pan. Use a rubber spatula to flip the turkey halfway through cooking, keeping as much of the Parmesan crust as possible on the nuggets. Serve the turkey nuggets with the slaw and the remaining dressing on the side.

NUTRITION FACTS PER SERVING (4 NUGGETS + ¾ CUP/150 G SLAW + ¼ CUP/60 ML DRESSING):
Total carbs: 10.4 g | Fiber: 3.6 g | Net carbs: 6.8 g | Protein: 45.9 g | Fat: 54.2 g | Calories: 709 kcal
MACRONUTRIENT RATIO: Calories from carbs (4%), protein (26%), fat (70%)

Mexican Chicken Bowls

4 SERVINGS
HANDS-ON TIME: 20 MINUTES
OVERALL TIME: 1 HOUR 30 MINUTES

MARINATED CHICKEN

1.3 pounds (600 g) chicken breasts, cut into 1½-inch (4-cm) pieces

2 tablespoons (30 ml) extra-virgin olive oil

1 tablespoon (15 ml) fresh lemon juice

1 tablespoon (15 ml) white wine vinegar

1 tablespoon (5 g/0.2 oz) dried oregano

½ teaspoon chipotle powder

½ teaspoon sea salt

¼ teaspoon black pepper

AVOCADO-FETA SALSA

3 tablespoons (45 ml) extra-virgin olive oil

2 tablespoons (30 ml) fresh lime juice

1 clove garlic, crushed

1 large (200 g/7.1 oz) avocado, pitted, peeled, and diced

2 cups (300 g/10.6 oz) halved cherry or chopped regular tomatoes

1 small (60/2.1 oz) red onion, sliced

2 teaspoons dried oregano

2 tablespoons (8 g/0.3 oz) chopped fresh cilantro or parsley

¾ cup (113 g/4 oz) crumbled feta cheese or queso fresco

Sea salt and black pepper, to taste

1 tablespoon (15 g/0.5 oz) ghee or duck fat

1 head (200 g/7.1 oz) romaine

Optional: Salsa verde, for serving

Keto flu can strike when your body is learning to use fat instead of carbs for energy. But eating foods rich in electrolytes like potassium and magnesium can help relieve keto flu symptoms such as headaches, fatigue, and nausea. This potassium-rich meal is a great option if you're just starting to eat keto: Make these Mexican Chicken Bowls ahead of time so that a nourishing lunch is within easy reach.

TO MAKE THE CHICKEN: Place the chicken pieces in a bowl. Add the olive oil, lemon juice, vinegar, oregano, chipotle powder, salt, and pepper. Mix until well coated, cover, and let the chicken marinate in the fridge for at least 1 hour, or overnight.

TO MAKE THE AVOCADO-FETA SALSA: In a bowl, combine the olive oil, lime juice, and garlic. Place the avocado, tomatoes, onion, herbs, and feta in a bowl, and pour over the prepared oil mixture. Season with salt and pepper to taste. Place in the fridge while you cook the chicken, or store covered for up to 2 days (but best served fresh).

Heat a large skillet greased with the ghee over medium-high heat. Add the marinated chicken pieces and cook until they are browned on all sides and cooked through, about 10 minutes.

To serve, fill 2 to 3 lettuce leaves with some avocado-feta salsa and serve with the chicken and, optionally, salsa verde. Leftover chicken and salsa verde can be stored in an airtight container in the fridge for up to 4 days.

NUTRITION FACTS PER SERVING (¼ CHICKEN + AVOCADO-FETA SALSA): Total carbs: 13.5 g | Fiber: 6.8 g | Net carbs: 6.7 g | Protein: 38 g | Fat: 48.3 g | Calories: 635 kcal
MACRONUTRIENT RATIO: Calories from carbs (4%), protein (25%), fat (71%)

Ham & Cheese Bread Rolls

15 SERVINGS
HANDS-ON TIME: 15 MINUTES
OVERALL TIME: 1 HOUR

DRY INGREDIENTS

1½ cups (150 g/5.3 oz) almond flour

½ cup (75 g/2.7 oz) firmly packed
  flax meal

½ cup (60 g/2.1 oz) coconut flour

⅓ cup (40 g/2.8 oz) psyllium husk
  powder

1 tablespoon (7 g/0.3 oz) onion
  powder

1 teaspoon baking soda

2 teaspoons cream of tartar

1 teaspoon sea salt

WET INGREDIENTS

6 large pastured egg whites (reserve
  2 yolks for egg wash and the
  remaining 4 yolks for another
  recipe; see Notes)

2 large pastured eggs

2 cups (480 ml) boiling water

FILLING & TOPPING

7 oz (198 g) sliced provolone or
  Monterey Jack cheese

9 oz (255 g) sliced quality ham

2 large egg yolks, reserved from wet
  ingredients above

1 tablespoon (15 ml) water

Optional: Seeds of your choice
  for topping (sesame, poppy,
  sunflower, or caraway)

These pretty, roulade-style roll-ups are based on my popular keto bread recipe, which I roll out thinly, then fill with ham and cheese. They're delicious hot or cold, so they're perfect for tossing into your lunchbox, either with or without a side of Marinara Sauce (page 166). They're very high in fiber, though, so be sure to drink plenty of water with them!

Preheat the oven to 350°F (175°C, or gas mark 4).

TO MAKE THE DOUGH: Place all of the dry ingredients into an electric mixer and mix until well combined. Add the wet ingredients. Start with the egg whites and eggs, and process well. Pour in the boiling water, and process until well combined. This shouldn't take more than a few seconds; avoid overmixing the dough.

Lay out a sheet of parchment paper or a silicone mat on a flat work surface. Transfer the dough to the parchment paper and flatten with your hands into a thin rectangle, about ½ inch (1 cm) thick. The sides should be about 16 inches (40 cm) long.

Lay the cheese slices over the dough and top with the ham slices, leaving a ½- to 1-inch (1- to 2.5-cm) margin along each side. Roll up the dough and cut it into thirds. Then cut each third into 5 pieces to create 15 equal servings. Place all the rolls on a large baking tray. Lay the first and last slices cut-side up.

To make the egg wash, mix the egg yolks with the water and brush on top of the rolls. Optionally, sprinkle with seeds. Transfer the tray to the oven and bake for 40 to 45 minutes, until golden brown. When done, remove the tray from the oven and leave the rolls to cool. Serve as a side or add to your lunchbox. Store in the fridge for up to 3 days or freeze for up to 3 months.

NUTRITION FACTS PER SERVING (1 ROLL): Total carbs: 7.8 g | Fiber: 5.2 g | Net carbs: 2.6 g | Protein: 12.8 g | Fat: 13.3 g | Calories: 191 kcal
MACRONUTRIENT RATIO: Calories from carbs (6%), protein (28%), fat (66%)

NOTES:

- I get the best results with whole psyllium husks that I "powder" myself in a coffee grinder. I've tried many different psyllium husk powder products and they don't always work for keto bread: they are too dense and often result in purple discoloration.
- Keto bread tends to get wet on the bottom. If these rolls get soggy, simply crisp them up in the oven just before serving.
- Don't waste the egg yolks! Keep them for other recipes, like Mayonnaise (page 163), Snickerdoodle Crème Brûlée (page 153), Boston Cream Pie (page 150) or Hollandaise Sauce (page 22).

Spiced Coconut Granola Bars

8 SERVINGS
HANDS-ON TIME: 10 MINUTES
OVERALL TIME: 30 MINUTES

- ½ cup (35 g/1.2 oz) unsweetened dried shredded coconut
- ½ cup (30 g / 1.1 oz) unsweetned dried flaked coconut
- ¼ cup (35 g/1.2 oz) almonds
- ¼ cup (35 g/1.2 oz) macadamia nuts
- ¼ cup (30 g/1.1 oz) pecans
- ¼ cup (30 g/1.1 oz) chia seeds
- ¼ cup (30 g/1.1 oz) pumpkin seeds
- ⅓ cup (35 g/1.2 oz) whey protein, egg white protein powder, or collagen
- 1 tablespoon (7 g/0.25 oz) pumpkin pie spice mix
- ¼ cup (40 g/1.4 oz) powdered erythritol
- Pinch salt
- 2 large egg whites
- ¾ cup (185 g/6.6 oz) coconut butter
- 2 tablespoons (30 g) virgin coconut oil or butter
- ½ cup (120 ml) coconut milk
- 15 to 20 drops liquid stevia

When life gets busy, lunch breaks tend to fall by the wayside. And if you find yourself in your car or on your feet all day, you might not even have access to a fridge, which limits your lunch options in a big way. These Spiced Coconut Granola Bars are a lifesaver when you're in a pinch: keep a couple in your bag so you won't be tempted to resort to high-carb or processed treats.

Preheat the oven to 325°F (160°C, or gas mark 3). Place the shredded and flaked coconut in a large mixing bowl. Roughly chop the almonds, macadamia nuts, and pecans. Add the nuts, then the chia and pumpkin seeds, protein powder (plain or vanilla), pumpkin spice mix, powdered erythritol, and salt. Mix until well combined.

Put the egg whites, coconut butter, coconut oil, coconut milk, and liquid stevia into a small saucepan and gently heat until melted and combined. Pour the coconut mixture into the dry mixture and combine well.

Line an 8 × 8 inch (20 × 20 cm) pan with parchment paper or use a silicone pan. Scoop the mixture into the dish and spread it out evenly using a spatula. Bake for about 30 minutes, or until golden. When done, remove the dish from the oven and place it on a rack to cool. Let the granola cool completely before cutting into 8 bars. Store at room temperature in an airtight container for up to 5 days or refrigerate for up to 10 days.

NOTE:
You can make your own pumpkin pie spice mix. To get ½ cup (48 g/1.7 oz) pumpkin pie spice mix, combine ¼ cup (28 g/1 oz) Ceylon cinnamon, 2 tablespoons (11 g/0.4 oz) ground ginger, 2 teaspoons ground nutmeg, 1 teaspoon ground cloves, and 1 teaspoon ground allspice. Optionally, add ½ teaspoon ground cardamom and ½ teaspoon ground mace. Store in an airtight container in your cupboard.

NUTRITION FACTS PER BAR: Total carbs: 12.7 g | Fiber: 8.5 g | Net carbs: 4.2 g | Protein: 11.3 g | Fat: 33.9 g | Calories: 377 kcal
MACRONUTRIENT RATIO: Calories from carbs (5%), protein (12%), fat (83%)

CHEESE-STUFFED GREEK BIFTEKI, PAGE 137

KETO KUNG PAO CHICKEN, PAGE 114

PORK SCHNITZEL WITH ZESTY SLAW, PAGE 116
BELOW: SALISBURY STEAK WITH QUICK MASH, PAGE 132

CHAPTER 6

HIGH-FAT
Dinners
ALL WEEK LONG

HEALTHY FISH STICKS WITH TARTAR SAUCE, PAGE 97

STEAK FAJITAS WITH SALSA VERDE, PAGE 133

BEEF BOURGUIGNON, PAGE 131
BELOW: CAJUN ANDOUILLE GUMBO, PAGE 101

DINNER CAN BE A MOVABLE FEAST—PUN VERY MUCH INTENDED!—depending on the day of the week. Harried weekdays call for quick-prep options that take minutes to make—or even microwaved leftovers, if you end up getting home late from work. On weekends, though, when you have the luxury of extra time, you might want to treat yourself to a meal that takes a bit longer to prepare.

This chapter has plenty of ideas for all kinds of filling, balanced keto mains. It's got vegetarian options, like the creamy-cheesy Broccoli & Mushroom Alfredo Casserole on page 94, or vegetarian keto Masala Cauli-Rice with Grilled Halloumi on page 96. (If you're dying for Indian takeout, it's sure to scratch your itch.) Keto Kung Pao Chicken (page 114) and the Healthy Deconstructed Hamburgers (page 127) are also fun, low-carb riffs on takeout classics, while Steak Fajitas with Avocado Salsa Verde (page 133) come together amazingly quickly—and that's a gift when it's 7 p.m. and you're absolutely starving. Traditional dishes like Coq au Vin (page 105) and Roast Duck with Braised Cabbage (page 113) do require a little more time. But trust me: They're so worth it.

TURKEY SOUVLAKI WITH SUPERGREENS SALAD, PAGE 115

Greek Briam

6 SERVINGS
HANDS-ON TIME: 15 MINUTES
OVERALL TIME: 45 MINUTES

¼ cup (55 g/1.9 oz) ghee or extra-
virgin olive oil
1 small (70 g/2.5 oz) yellow onion,
sliced
2 cloves garlic, minced
1 medium (250 g/8.8 oz) eggplant,
cut into ½-inch (1-cm) pieces
½ medium (150 g/3.5 oz) broccoli,
roughly chopped
½ medium (250 g/8.8 oz)
cauliflower, roughly chopped
1 medium (120 g/4.2 oz) green bell
pepper, sliced
3 medium (300 g/10.6 oz) tomatoes,
roughly chopped
¼ cup (60 ml) water or vegetable
stock
2 small (300 g/10.6 oz) zucchini,
sliced
¼ cup (15 g/0.5 oz) chopped parsley,
divided
1 tablespoon (4 g/0.1 oz) fresh
chopped oregano or 1 teaspoon
dried oregano
¼ teaspoon fine sea salt, or to taste
Freshly ground black pepper, to
taste
1½ cups (225 g/8 oz) crumbled feta
cheese
½ cup (120 ml) extra-virgin olive oil

One of the most persistent myths about the ketogenic diet is that it doesn't include vegetables. Nothing could be further from the truth! Take *briam*, a traditional Greek vegetarian dish that's a distant relative of French ratatouille (see Ratatouille Soup, page 64). It's keto-friendly, highly nutritious, full of low-carb vegetables, and makes a wonderful weekday dinner (or weekend lunch).

In a large heavy-based casserole dish greased with ghee, cook the onion over medium-high heat for 5 to 8 minutes, until lightly browned. Add the garlic and eggplant, and cover with a lid. Lower the heat to medium-low and cook for 3 to 5 minutes.

Add the broccoli and cauliflower, and cook, covered, for 3 to 5 minutes. Add the pepper, tomatoes, and water. Stir and cover with a lid. Cook for another 5 minutes, add the zucchini, and stir to combine. Cook, covered, for 5 to 10 minutes, or until the zucchini is tender.

Preheat the broiler. Mix in the parsley (leave some parsley for garnish), oregano, salt, and pepper. Top with the feta cheese. Place under the broiler and cook on high for about 5 minutes, or until the feta is lightly browned. Leave to cool for 5 minutes. Garnish with more parsley and drizzle with the olive oil. Eat hot or cold. Once cooled, refrigerate for up to 5 days.

NUTRITION FACTS PER SERVING: Total carbs: 13.9 g | Fiber: 4.6 g | Net carbs: 9.3 g | Protein: 8.7 g | Fat: 35.8 g | Calories: 400 kcal
MACRONUTRIENT RATIO: Calories from carbs (9%), protein (9%), fat (82%)

Broccoli & Mushroom Alfredo Casserole

6 SERVINGS
HANDS-ON TIME: 10 MINUTES
OVERALL TIME: 1 HOUR

2 large (800 g/1.8 lb) broccoli

¼ cup (55 g/1.9 oz) ghee or extra-virgin olive oil

1 small (70 g/2.5 oz) yellow onion, chopped

1 cup (240 ml) heavy whipping cream

2 cloves garlic, minced

1 teaspoon dried Italian herbs

3 cups (210 g/7.4 oz) sliced white or brown mushrooms

1½ cups (135 g/4.8 oz) grated Parmesan cheese or hard cheese of choice, divided

Salt and pepper, to taste

I used to love fettucine Alfredo, with its creamy sauce coating each long strand of pasta. Of course, pasta is too high in carbs to be part of a ketogenic lifestyle, but cheesy Alfredo sauce is certainly keto-friendly. In this simple vegetarian casserole, broccoli florets soak up the sauce beautifully, and mushrooms add lots of meaty texture and earthy flavor.

Preheat the oven to 360°F (180°C, or gas mark 4). Cut the broccoli into florets. Peel and chop the broccoli stalks. Bring a saucepan filled with salted water to a boil. Add the broccoli and cook for 3 to 4 minutes, until crisp-tender. Drain and set aside to let any excess water drip off.

Grease a large skillet or casserole dish with the ghee. Add the onion and cook over medium-high heat for 5 to 8 minutes, until lightly browned. Add the cream, garlic, and Italian herbs. Bring to a boil and add the mushrooms. Cook, uncovered, for 5 to 7 minutes, and add the Parmesan cheese (reserve some for topping) and blanched broccoli. Taste and season with salt and pepper.

Take off the heat and top with the reserved Parmesan cheese. Transfer to the oven and bake for 25 to 30 minutes, or until crisped up and lightly browned. Serve immediately, or let it cool and place in an airtight container. Refrigerate for up to 5 days.

NUTRITION FACTS PER SERVING: Total carbs: 13.2 g | Fiber: 4.1 g | Net carbs: 9.1 g | Protein: 13.8 g | Fat: 30.8 g | Calories: 377 kcal
MACRONUTRIENT RATIO: Calories from carbs (10%), protein (15%), fat (75%)

Masala Cauli-Rice with Grilled Halloumi

4 SERVINGS
HANDS-ON TIME: 20 MINUTES
OVERALL TIME: 20 MINUTES

⅓ cup (73 g/2.6 oz) ghee or virgin coconut oil, divided

1 small (70 g/2.5 oz) yellow onion, chopped

1 clove garlic, minced

1 small (5 g/0.2 oz) red or green chile pepper, chopped, seeds removed

½ teaspoon garam masala

½ teaspoon ground turmeric

½ teaspoon ground cumin

½ teaspoon ground coriander

⅛ to ¼ teaspoon chili powder

6 cups (720 g/1.6 lb) plain Cauliflower Rice (page 13)

1 medium (120 g/4.2 oz) tomato, chopped

Sea salt and black pepper, to taste

11.3 ounces (320 g) Halloumi cheese, about 80 g/2.8 oz per serving

Vegetarian keto masala sounds almost too good to be true, so don't take my word for it: make it yourself next time you're craving Indian takeout! In this version, Indian-spiced cauliflower rice takes the place of the regular, starchy variety, and chewy Halloumi cheese offers protein and texture. (Just be sure to let the Halloumi brown well before serving.)

Grease a large skillet with the ghee (reserve about 1 tablespoon [15 g] for cooking the Halloumi). Cook the onion over medium-high heat for 5 to 7 minutes, until lightly browned and fragrant. Then add the garlic and chile. Add all the spices, cook for a minute, and then add the cauli-rice. Cook for 5 minutes, stirring frequently. Then add the tomato and cook for another 2 to 3 minutes, or until the cauli-rice is tender. Season with salt and pepper to taste. Set aside and keep warm.

Grease a skillet (regular or griddle) with the remaining ghee. Slice the Halloumi into about ½-inch (1-cm) slices. Add the Halloumi to the skillet, and cook over medium-high heat on both sides for 2 to 3 minutes. Do not flip too early: let the cheese become crisp and brown to prevent it from breaking. When done, serve immediately with the prepared masala cauli-rice. To store, let it cool and refrigerate in an airtight container for up to 5 days. Reheat before serving.

NUTRITION FACTS PER SERVING: Total carbs: 14.1 g | Fiber: 4.6 g | Net carbs: 9.5 g | Protein: 20.1 g | Fat: 40.7 g | Calories: 491 kcal
MACRONUTRIENT RATIO: Calories from carbs (8%), protein (17%), fat (75%)

Healthy Fish Sticks with Tartar Sauce

4 SERVINGS
HANDS-ON TIME: 15 MINUTES
OVERALL TIME: 45 MINUTES

FISH STICKS

1 medium (15 g/0.5 oz) spring onion

4 cod fillets, skinned and deboned
  (600 g/1.3 lb)

2 tablespoons (24 g/0.8 oz) coconut flour

1 large egg, beaten

1 tablespoon (15 ml) freshly squeezed
  lemon juice

½ teaspoon salt

Freshly ground black pepper, to taste

3 tablespoons (20 g/0.7 oz) flax meal

⅓ cup (30 g/1.1 oz) grated Parmesan
  cheese or pork rinds

2 tablespoons (30 g/1.1 oz) ghee, melted,
  or coconut oil

SLAW

¼ medium (250 g/8.8 oz) green or white
  cabbage

¼ small (100 g/3.5 oz) red cabbage

½ fennel bulb (120 g/4.1 oz)

1 medium (15 g/0.5 oz) spring onion

¼ cup (55 g/1.9 oz) Mayonnaise (page 163)

1 teaspoon Dijon mustard

Salt and freshly ground black pepper,
  to taste

TARTAR SAUCE

½ cup (110 g/3.9 oz) Mayonnaise (page 163)

1 pickle (65 g/2.3 oz)

1 tablespoon (15 ml) freshly squeezed
  lemon juice

Salt, to taste

Your favorite childhood meal is all grown up! These low-carb fish sticks are a far cry from the breaded, processed versions you loved as a kid. They're made with fresh cod, and are best served with a homemade tartar sauce and a side of cabbage and fennel slaw. And they don't take long to whip up, so they make a great midweek dinner for the whole family.

TO MAKE THE FISH STICKS: Preheat the oven to 400°F (200°C, or gas mark 6). Slice the spring onion. Place the cod in a blender and pulse until smooth. Transfer the blended cod to a bowl and add the coconut flour, egg, lemon juice, and the spring onion. Season with salt and black pepper and mix until well combined.

Prepare the breading by mixing the flax meal, Parmesan cheese, salt, and black pepper in a bowl.

Using your hands, form 12 fish sticks (3 per serving). Roll each one in the breading until completely coated. Place on a baking sheet lined with parchment paper and drizzle with the melted ghee. Transfer to the oven and bake for 25 to 30 minute, or until crispy and golden.

TO MAKE THE SLAW: Wash the cabbage and fennel. Using a sharp knife, finely slice the cabbage, fennel bulb, and spring onion, or put all three in a food processor and shred using a grating blade. Set the shredded vegetables in a mixing bowl. Add the mayo and Dijon mustard and season with salt and black pepper. Set aside.

TO MAKE THE TARTAR SAUCE: Mix all the ingredients in a small bowl.

When the fish sticks are done, remove them from the oven and let them cool slightly. Serve with the slaw and tartar sauce.

NUTRITION FACTS PER SERVING (3 FISH STICKS + 1 CUP/200 G SLAW+ 3 TABLESPOONS/45 G TARTAR SAUCE):
Total carbs: 13.1 g | Fiber: 6 g | Net carbs: 7.1 g | Protein: 35.1 g | Fat: 49.2 g | Calories: 631 kcal
MACRONUTRIENT RATIO: Calories from carbs (5%), protein (23%), fat (72%)

Sushi: Spicy Tuna Rolls

4 SERVINGS
HANDS-ON TIME: 20 MINUTES
OVERALL TIME: 35 MINUTES

SUSHI

½ small (56 g/2 oz) cucumber

1 large (200 g/7.1 oz) avocado

1 medium (15 g/0.5 oz) spring onion

1½ cups (220 g/8.1 oz) canned tuna, drained

2 cloves garlic, crushed

1 teaspoon grated ginger

2 teaspoons toasted sesame oil

¼ cup (55 g/1.9 oz) Mayonnaise (page 163), divided

2 teaspoons Sriracha

½ teaspoon salt, or to taste

4 cups (480 g/16.9 oz) uncooked plain Cauliflower Rice (page 13)

4 nori seaweed sheets

4 large (60 g/2.1 oz) lettuce leaves

TOPPING

¼ cup (55 g/1.9 oz) Mayonnaise (page 163)

1 teaspoon Sriracha

Salt and cayenne pepper, to taste

2 tablespoons (16 g/0.6 oz) sesame seeds

There really isn't anything that cauliflower rice *can't* do. The proof? These low-carb sushi rolls, which are stuffed with a mixture of tuna, avocado, garlic, ginger, and sesame. They're one of my favorite workday lunches: it's so easy to grab one when you're on the go, or when you're eating at your desk.

TO MAKE THE SUSHI: Wash, peel, and slice the cucumber into long, thin stalks. Halve, deseed, and peel the avocado, and cut into long slices. Wash and slice the spring onion.

In a bowl, combine the drained tuna, sliced spring onion, crushed garlic, ginger, and sesame oil. Add 2 tablespoons (28 g/1 oz) of the mayonnaise, Sriracha, and salt. Mix until well combined.

In another bowl, add the remaining 2 tablespoons (28 g/1 oz) mayonnaise to the cauli-rice, and season with salt. Mix until well combined. The mayo will act as glue for the "rice."

Top each nori sheet with the cauli-rice. Make sure the cauli-rice doesn't cover the whole sheet; leave 1 to 2 inches (2.5 to 5 cm) on the sides. Top each sheet with a lettuce leaf, one-fourth of the tuna mixture, one-fourth of a sliced avocado, and one-fourth of the cucumber. Make sure you place the filling on the top half of the nori so you can wrap it easily. Roll it up to the edge, wet the nori with a few drops of water, and seal well. Place the rolls with the sealed side down to keep the wraps tight. Leave to rest for 10 to 15 minutes before slicing, or place in the fridge.

TO MAKE THE TOPPING: In a small bowl, mix the mayonnaise with the Sriracha and season with salt and cayenne pepper to taste. Dry-roast the sesame seeds in a small skillet over low heat for a minute, or until golden. Cut each roll into 8 pieces and sprinkle with the toasted sesame seeds. Serve with the spicy mayonnaise.

NUTRITION FACTS PER SERVING (1 UNCUT ROLL + 1 TABLESPOON/15 G/0.5 OZ SPICY MAYO): Total carbs: 15.6 g | Fiber: 8.4 g | Net carbs: 7.2 g | Protein: 21.5 g | Fat: 44.3 g | Calories: 523 kcal
MACRONUTRIENT RATIO: Calories from carbs (5%), protein (17%), fat (78%)

Harissa Fish Tray Bake

6 SERVINGS
HANDS-ON TIME: 15 MINUTES
OVERALL TIME: 50 MINUTES

1 recipe (160 g/5.6 oz) Spicy Harissa Butter (page 14)

1 pack (200 g/7.1 oz) fresh spinach or chard

1 medium (300 g/10.6 oz) eggplant, roughly chopped

1 medium (400 g/14.1 oz) cauliflower, sliced

1 medium (110 g/3.9 oz) white onion, sliced

4 medium (300 g/10.6 oz) tomatoes, chopped

2 tablespoons (8 g/0.3 oz) chopped fresh parsley or cilantro

6 boneless (540 g/1.2 lb) sea bass fillets

Salt and pepper, to taste

3 tablespoons (45 ml) extra-virgin olive oil

Short on time this evening? Tray bakes are so easy to put together: they require only minimum prep, and this one takes barely more than half an hour in the oven. My homemade Spicy Harissa Butter (page 14) is the perfect flavor booster for the roasted vegetables and tender fish in this Moroccan-inspired, one-pan meal.

Melt the harissa butter in a small saucepan. Preheat the oven to 400°F (200°C, or gas mark 6).

Place the spinach into a baking dish large enough to hold all of the ingredients. Top with the eggplant, cauliflower, onion, tomatoes, and parsley (reserve some parsley for garnish). Drizzle with half the melted butter, place in the oven, and bake for about 20 minutes. Then add the sea bass fillets skin-side up, and drizzle them with the remaining butter.

Bake for 12 to 15 minutes. Garnish with the reserved parsley, and season with salt and pepper to taste. Drizzle with the olive oil and serve, or let cool and refrigerate for up to 4 days.

NUTRITION FACTS PER SERVING (1 FILLET + ⅙ VEGETABLES): Total carbs: 12.7 g | Fiber: 5.1 g | Net carbs: 7.6 g | Protein: 20.9 g | Fat: 26.9 g | Calories: 366 kcal
MACRONUTRIENT RATIO: Calories from carbs (9%), protein (23%), fat (68%)

Cajun Andouille Gumbo

8 SERVINGS
HANDS-ON TIME: 15 MINUTES
OVERALL TIME: 55 MINUTES

¼ cup (55 g/1.9 oz) ghee or duck fat

1 medium (110 g/3.9 oz) yellow onion, chopped

4 cloves garlic, minced

1 medium (120 g/4.2 oz) green bell pepper, sliced

2 large (128 g/4.5 oz) celery stalks, sliced

14.1 ounces (400 g) canned chopped tomatoes

4 cups (950 ml) fish stock or chicken stock

1 teaspoon dried thyme

1 teaspoon dried oregano

1 teaspoon ancho chile powder or smoked paprika

¼ teaspoon cayenne pepper

14.1 ounces (400 g) okra, trimmed and roughly chopped, or chopped frozen okra

1.1 pounds (500 g) andouille sausages, Mexican chorizo sausages, or kielbasa, cut into 1-inch (2.5-cm) slices

1½ pounds (680 g) raw shrimp, peeled

Salt and pepper, to taste

Chopped fresh parsley, chives, or spring onions, for garnish

Gumbo is a traditional Creole stew, made with a fish stock base and topped up with vegetables, seafood, and andouille sausage. My version takes just 40 minutes to make, but it tastes like it's been simmering on the stovetop all day. Serve it to a hungry crowd with Cauliflower Rice (page 13) or Sourdough Keto Buns (page 10). They'll love you for it!

Grease a large heavy-based saucepan or Dutch oven with the ghee. Add the onion and cook over medium-high heat for 5 to 8 minutes, until lightly browned. Add the garlic, green pepper, and celery. Cook for 2 minutes, then add the tomatoes, stock, thyme, oregano, ancho powder, cayenne pepper, okra, and andouille sausage. Bring to a boil, reduce the heat, and simmer, uncovered, for 25 to 30 minutes, or until the okra is tender and the gumbo has slightly thickened.

Add the shrimp and cook for 2 to 3 more minutes and then take off the heat. Season with salt and pepper to taste and garnish with fresh herbs. Serve immediately. To store, let it cool, and refrigerate for up to 4 days or freeze for up to 3 months.

NOTE:
If you have any leftover shrimp shells, use them to make a batch of seafood stock! Not a fan of shrimp? Swap them for sliced chicken thighs!

NUTRITION FACTS PER SERVING: Total carbs: 11.2 g | Fiber: 3.9 g | Net carbs: 7.3 g | Protein: 26.6 g | Fat: 22.6 g | Calories: 349 kcal
MACRONUTRIENT RATIO: Calories from carbs (9%), protein (31%), fat (60%)

Thai Curry Chicken Tray Bake

4 SERVINGS
HANDS-ON TIME: 15 MINUTES
OVERALL TIME: 35 MINUTES

1 medium (200 g/7.1 oz) bok choy, leaves separated

1 small (70 g/2.5 oz) onion, sliced

1 small (74 g/2.6 oz) green pepper, sliced

1 small (400 g/1.1 lb) cauliflower, sliced

2 cups (200 g/7.1 oz) green beans

8 small (900 g/2 lbs) bone-in, skin-on chicken thighs

Sea salt and black pepper, to taste

1 tablespoon (15 g/0.5 oz) ghee or duck fat

1 cup (240 ml) coconut milk

2 tablespoons (30 ml) fresh lime juice

½ recipe (73 g/2.6 oz) Thai Curry Butter (page 14), sliced

2 tablespoons (8 g/0.3 oz) chopped fresh cilantro

This is another one-pan tray bake that's great when you need a quick fix for dinner, with minimal prep and cleanup. Chicken thighs with crispy skin (the best part!) are baked with homemade Thai Curry Butter (page 14) and a variety of low-carb veggies. If you can't eat dairy, simply use coconut oil or duck fat to make the flavored butter.

Preheat the oven to 400°F (200°C, or gas mark 6). Lay the bok choy leaves in a large baking tray. Add the onion, green pepper, cauliflower, and green beans.

Pat the chicken thighs dry with a paper towel, and season with salt and pepper. Heat a large skillet greased with the ghee. Once hot, add the chicken thighs, skin-side down, and cook in batches for about 5 minutes, or until the skin is golden and crispy. Flip over and cook for just 1 minute more.

Place the chicken on top of the vegetables in the baking dish, skin-side up. Deglaze the skillet by pouring the coconut milk and lime juice into it and add half of the flavored butter, then pour the mixture over the vegetables in the tray. Top with the crisped-up chicken thighs and top each chicken thigh with a slice of the remaining flavored butter.

Bake for 20 to 25 minutes. The chicken is done when an instant-read thermometer inserted into the thickest part of the thigh reads 165°F (75°C). Top with the cilantro and serve. Crispy chicken thighs are best served immediately, but they can be stored in the fridge for up to 4 days.

NUTRITION FACTS PER SERVING (2 THIGHS + ¼ VEGETABLES): Total carbs: 13.3 g | Fiber: 4.4 g | Net carbs: 8.9 g | Protein: 34.7 g | Fat: 34 g | Calories: 484 kcal
MACRONUTRIENT RATIO: Calories from carbs (7%), protein (29%), fat (64%)

Coq au Vin

8 SERVINGS
HANDS-ON TIME: 20 MINUTES
OVERALL TIME: 1 HOUR 15 MINUTES

BOUQUET GARNI

4 bay leaves

4 thyme sprigs

1 teaspoon black peppercorns

Small bunch parsley

CHICKEN

6 large (180 g/6.4 oz) slices bacon, chopped

8 large (1.6 kg/3.5 lb) bone-in chicken thighs, trimmed of excess fat and skin (or use 1.2 kg/2.7 lb boneless chicken)

Sea salt and ground black pepper, to taste

2 tablespoons (30 g/1.1 oz) ghee or duck fat, divided

5.3 ounces (150 g) baby onions, peeled

2 large (128 g/4.5 oz) celery stalks, sliced

2 cloves garlic, minced

4 cups (300 g/10.6 oz) sliced white mushrooms

1 bottle (750 ml) dry red wine, or 2 ¾ cups (656 ml) Bone Broth (page 160), plus 3 to 6 tablespoons (45 to 90 ml) red wine vinegar

1 cup (240 ml) water or chicken stock

2 tablespoons (30 g/1.1 oz) unsweetened tomato paste

Fresh parsley, for garnish

Coq au vin, a beloved French bistro classic, often calls for flour and high-carb vegetables, so it's usually off-menu if you're eating low-carb. But feel free to say yes to this keto version!

TO MAKE THE BOUQUET GARNI: Place all the herbs in a piece of cheesecloth and tie with unwaxed kitchen string.

TO MAKE THE CHICKEN: Place the bacon slices in a large casserole dish and add ½ cup (120 ml) of water. Cook over medium-high heat until the water starts to boil. Reduce the heat to medium and cook for about 10 minutes, until the water evaporates and the bacon is crisped up. Use a slotted spoon to transfer the bacon to a plate and set aside.

Season the chicken thighs with salt on all sides. Grease the casserole dish where you cooked the bacon with half of the ghee and add the chicken thighs in a single layer, to skin-side down. Cook over medium-high heat for 5 to 8 minutes. Turn on the other side and cook for another 3 minutes. Remove the chicken from the pan and set aside on a plate.

Grease the casserole dish with the remaining ghee and add the whole onions. Cook for 5 to 8 minutes, turning occasionally. Add the celery, garlic, and mushrooms, and cook for 1 minute. Pour in the wine and bring to a boil, scraping the browned bits from the bottom of the pan with a spatula. Add the water, tomato paste, and bouquet garni. Mix until combined, and season with salt and pepper.

Place the chicken, skin-side up, back in the pan and spoon the pan juices over the chicken. Cover with a lid and cook for 25 to 30 minutes. Add the crisped-up bacon and stir into the sauce. Place the casserole dish under a broiler to crisp up for about 5 minutes. Remove from the oven and let it cool for a few minutes. Serve with Cauliflower Rice (page 13) or steamed low-carb veggies. To store, let it cool, and refrigerate for up to 3 days.

NUTRITION FACTS PER SERVING (1 THIGH PLUS VEGETABLES): Total carbs: 6.4 g | Fiber: 1.1 g | Net carbs: 5.3 g | Protein: 25.8 g | Fat: 50.8 g | Calories: 653 kcal
MACRONUTRIENT RATIO: Calories from carbs (4%), protein (17%), fat (79%)

Butter Chicken

6 SERVINGS
HANDS-ON TIME: 30 MINUTES
OVERALL TIME: 3 HOURS

MARINATED CHICKEN

6 small (2 lb/900 g) chicken breasts
¾ cup (188 g/6.6 oz) 5% full-fat yogurt
2 tablespoons (30 ml) fresh lemon juice
1 tablespoon (7 g/0.2 oz) ground turmeric
1 tablespoon (6 g/0.2 oz) garam masala
1 tablespoon (5 g/0.2 oz) ground cumin
1 teaspoon ground cinnamon

STEW

¼ cup (55 g/1.9 oz) ghee or duck fat
1 small (70 g/2.5 oz) yellow onion, finely chopped
2 cloves garlic, minced
2 tablespoons (12 g/0.4 oz) grated fresh ginger
1 to 2 medium (14 g/0.5 oz) red or green chiles, seeds removed, chopped
3 tablespoons (45 g/1.6 oz) unsweetened tomato paste
1 cup (240 ml) chicken stock or water
¼ cup (57 g/2 oz) butter
1 teaspoon sea salt
½ teaspoon black pepper
1¼ cups (300 ml) heavy whipping cream
Fresh cilantro, for garnish
Serving suggestions: Cauliflower Rice (page 13) or shirataki rice

Anything with the word "butter" in the title simply has to be delicious, right? Well, this mild Indian dish sure is. Pieces of chicken breast are bathed in a yogurt marinade before being cooked with ginger, spices, cream, and—you guessed it—butter. Once the chicken has been marinated, it's ready in just half an hour, so it's one of my go-to meals for busy weeknights.

TO MAKE THE CHICKEN: Cut the chicken into 1½-inch (4-cm) pieces. In a bowl, combine all the ingredients for the marinade. Add the chicken, cover with plastic wrap, and refrigerate for 2 hours or up to 24 hours.

TO MAKE THE STEW: Heat a large pot greased with the ghee over medium-high heat. Add the onion and cook for about 7 minutes, until fragrant and lightly browned. Add the garlic, ginger, and chiles. Cook for another 2 to 3 minutes. Add the marinated chicken, and cook for about 10 minutes, stirring frequently. Then add the tomato paste, chicken stock, butter, salt, and black pepper.

Bring to a boil, then reduce the heat to medium. Cook, uncovered, for 15 minutes. Pour in the cream and cook for another 5 to 10 minutes. Remove from the heat and let sit for 5 minutes. Serve with cilantro and cauliflower rice or shirataki rice.

NUTRITION FACTS PER SERVING (1 BREAST, DOES NOT INCLUDE SIDE): Total carbs: 7.3 g | Fiber: 1.2 g | Net carbs: 6.1 g | Protein: 37.2 g | Fat: 42.5 g | Calories: 569 kcal
MACRONUTRIENT RATIO: Calories from carbs (4%), protein (27%), fat (69%)

Crispy Chicken with Olives and Lemon

4 SERVINGS
HANDS-ON TIME: 15 MINUTES
OVERALL TIME: 1 HOUR

4 large (800 g/1.76 lb) bone-in chicken thighs, trimmed of excess fat and skin (or use 6 [600 g/ 1.3 lb] boneless chicken thighs)

½ teaspoon fine sea salt, or to taste

2 tablespoons (30 g/1.1 oz) ghee or duck fat, divided

1 small (70 g/2.5 oz) yellow onion, sliced

3 cloves garlic, minced

⅓ cup (80 ml) water or chicken stock

3 tablespoons (45 ml) fresh lemon juice

½ teaspoon dried thyme

½ teaspoon dried oregano

½ teaspoon dried rosemary

1 medium (400 g/14.1 oz) broccoli, cut into florets with stalks peeled and sliced

1 medium (200 g/7.1 oz) zucchini, sliced

¼ cup (35 g/1.2 oz) capers, drained

½ cup (50 g/1.8 oz) pitted olives of choice

1 whole (85 g/3 oz) lemon, sliced

Black pepper, to taste

Fresh parsley, for garnish

1 tablespoon (15 ml) extra-virgin olive oil

The combination of olives and fresh lemons is distilled sunshine; I can't get enough of it. Perk up a wintry day by making this Crispy Chicken with Olives and Lemon for dinner. It's much simpler than it tastes: you just sauté chicken thighs, then bake them with low-carb veggies, olives, lemon slices, and lots of fresh herbs.

Season the chicken thighs with salt on all sides. Heat a large skillet or casserole dish greased with 1 tablespoon (15 g/0.5 oz) of the ghee. Once hot, add the chicken thighs in a single layer, skin-side down. Cook over medium-high heat for 5 to 8 minutes. Turn onto the other side and cook for another 3 to 5 minutes. Remove the chicken from the pan and set aside on a plate.

Preheat the oven to 375°F (190°C, or gas mark 5). Grease the skillet with the remaining 1 tablespoon (15 g/0.5 oz) ghee. Add the onion and cook for 5 to 8 minutes, until lightly browned. Add the garlic, water, lemon juice, and herbs. Add the broccoli florets and stalks. Toss them in the juices, and cook, covered, over medium-low heat for about 3 minutes. Add the zucchini, capers, olives, and browned chicken thighs. Top with lemon slices and transfer to the oven. Cook, uncovered, for 15 to 20 minutes, or until the vegetables are tender.

When done, place on a cooling rack and remove the lemon slices. Season with pepper, garnish with fresh parsley, and drizzle with olive oil. Serve immediately, or let it cool and refrigerate for up to 3 days.

NUTRITION FACTS PER SERVING (1 THIGH + ¼ VEGETABLES): Total carbs: 12.4 g | Fiber: 4.4 g | Net carbs: 8 g | Protein: 25.4 g | Fat: 57.9 g | Calories: 667 kcal
MACRONUTRIENT RATIO: Calories from carbs (5%), protein (15%), fat (80%)

Chicken Piccata

4 SERVINGS
HANDS-ON TIME: 15 MINUTES
OVERALL TIME: 30 MINUTES

2 large (500 g/1.1 lb) skin-on boneless chicken breasts

3 tablespoons (45 ml) melted ghee, divided

1 small (70 g/2.5 oz) yellow onion, chopped

2 cloves garlic, minced

1 tablespoon (15 ml) white wine vinegar or apple cider vinegar

¼ cup (60 ml) fresh lemon juice

3 tablespoons (43 g/1.5 oz) butter

¼ cup (34 g/1.2 oz) capers, drained

2 tablespoons (8 g/0.3 oz) chopped fresh parsley, plus more for optional garnish

1 pound (450 g) fresh spinach

Sea salt and black pepper, to taste

¼ cup (60 ml) extra-virgin olive oil

Lemon slices, for garnish

This keto-friendly version of classic chicken piccata is a simple, elegant meal that comes together quickly—and that's a bonus when impromptu dinner guests turn up.

To butterfly the chicken breasts, place them on a chopping board. Placing your hand flat on top of one chicken breast, use a knife to slice into one side. Be careful not to cut all the way through to the other side. Open the breast so that it resembles a butterfly, about ½ inch (1 cm) thick.

Heat a large skillet greased with 1 tablespoon (15 ml) of the ghee over medium-high heat. Once hot, add the butterflied chicken, skin-side down. Cook undisturbed for 5 to 7 minutes. Rotate the pan halfway through to ensure even cooking. Then flip the chicken over and cook for another 2 to 3 minutes. When done, transfer to a plate, skin-side up.

Grease the pan with the remaining 2 tablespoons (30 ml) ghee, and add the onion. Cook for 5 to 7 minutes, or until golden brown. Add the garlic and cook for 1 minute more. To deglaze the pan, add the vinegar, lemon juice, and butter, scraping the browned bits from the bottom of the skillet. Add the capers and parsley. Return the cooked chicken to the pan and heat for 1 to 2 minutes. Remove from the heat and set aside.

To blanch the spinach, bring a large saucepan filled with salted water to a boil. Add the spinach and cook for 30 to 60 seconds, until wilted. Use a slotted spoon to transfer the spinach to a large bowl of ice water, then drain and squeeze out any excess water. Season with salt and pepper and drizzle with the olive oil. Serve with the crispy chicken and sauce. Garnish with lemon slices and more fresh parsley if desired. Crispy chicken is best served immediately, but can be refrigerated in an airtight container for up to 4 days.

NUTRITION FACTS PER SERVING (½ BREAST): Total carbs: 7.6 g | Fiber: 3.2 g | Net carbs: 4.4 g | Protein: 29.9 g | Fat: 45.5 g | Calories: 554 kcal
MACRONUTRIENT RATIO: Calories from carbs (3%), protein (22%), fat (75%)

Roast Duck with Braised Cabbage

4 SERVINGS
HANDS-ON TIME: 20 MINUTES
OVERALL TIME: 2 HOURS

DUCK

1 duck or 4 duck quarters (about 1.4 kg/3 lb, bones included)
¼ teaspoon salt
Freshly ground black pepper, to taste

BRAISED CABBAGE

½ medium (300 g/10.6 oz) head red cabbage, core removed
1 large (200 g/7.1 oz) turnip
1 small (70 g/2.5 oz) white onion
2 tablespoons (30 g/1.1 oz) ghee, lard, or duck fat
1½ cups (225 g/8 oz) sauerkraut, drained
¼ teaspoon ground cloves
2 tablespoons (30 ml) apple cider vinegar
½ to 1 cup (120 to 240 ml) chicken stock
Salt and freshly ground black pepper, to taste

Duck with red cabbage is a Central European classic, and it's especially wonderful in the autumn, when the weather turns cool and you crave dark meat, rich flavors, tangy sauerkraut, and low-carb root vegetables like turnips. Duck meat is keto-friendly if eaten with the skin on, so don't remove it before cooking.

TO MAKE THE DUCK: Preheat the oven to 400°F (200°C, or gas mark 6). Make sure you remove the giblets before cooking if using a whole duck.

Prick the duck's skin all over with the tip of a sharp knife and season with salt and black pepper. Place the duck on a rack in a roasting pan and roast for 1 hour 20 minutes to 1 hour 30 minutes (or 20 minutes per every pound [455 g] plus 20 minutes extra). When done, cover with aluminum foil and leave to rest for 15 minutes.

TO MAKE THE CABBAGE: Wash and slice the cabbage and peel and grate the turnip. Peel and finely slice the onion. Grease a large pot with the ghee and add the onion. Cook until translucent and then add the shredded cabbage, turnip, and drained sauerkraut. Add the ground cloves, vinegar, and chicken stock, and mix well. Season with salt and black pepper to taste. (If you're using a Dutch oven, you may not need any chicken stock, as only a small amount of water is lost during the cooking process.) Cover with a lid and cook over medium-low heat for about 30 minutes, or until tender. Stir a few times to prevent burning.

When done, quarter the duck. Pour the duck fat in with the cabbage and mix well. Place the cabbage on a serving plate and top with the duck.

NUTRITION FACTS PER SERVING: Total carbs: 13 g | Fiber: 4.5 g | Net carbs: 8.5 g | Protein: 25.9 g | Fat: 46.5 g | Calories: 568 kcal
MACRONUTRIENT RATIO: Calories from carbs (6%), protein (19%), fat (75%)

Keto Kung Pao Chicken

4 SERVINGS
HANDS-ON TIME: 20 MINUTES
OVERALL TIME: 1 HOUR

MARINADE

2 tablespoons (30 ml) toasted sesame oil

2 tablespoons (30 ml) fish sauce

1 tablespoon (15 ml) rice vinegar or white wine vinegar

2 tablespoons (30 ml) Shaoxing wine or dry white wine

2 tablespoons (30 ml) chicken stock

½ teaspoon sea salt

Ground black pepper, to taste

Optional: 1 tablespoon (10 g/0.4 oz) powdered erythritol or Swerve

CHICKEN

1.3 lb (600 g) boneless, skinless chicken thighs, sliced

3 tablespoons (45 g/1.6 oz) virgin coconut oil or ghee, divided

4 small (8 g/0.3 oz) dried Chinese chiles

½ cup (73 g/2.6 oz) blanched almonds

2 large (120 g/4.2 oz) celery stalks, sliced

1 large (160 g/5.6 oz) green bell pepper, sliced

1 medium (120 g/4.2 oz) red bell pepper, sliced

1 tablespoon (6 g/0.2 oz) fresh grated ginger

2 cloves garlic, minced

2 medium (30 g/1.1 oz) spring onions, sliced

Serving suggestion: Plain Cauliflower Rice (page 13), cooked in coconut oil

If you miss Chinese takeout, you've come to the right place. This low-carb kung pao chicken is even better than the real thing: it's got all of the flavor and none of the guilt. Essentially, it's marinated chicken cooked with low-carb vegetables, chiles, and almonds served over cauli-rice—and that's a well-balanced, keto-friendly meal you can feel good about.

TO MAKE THE MARINADE: Mix the sesame oil, fish sauce, vinegar, wine, chicken stock, salt, and pepper in a bowl. Optionally, add erythritol.

TO MAKE THE CHICKEN: Place the sliced chicken thighs in a medium bowl. Pour in half of the marinade, and let it sit for 20 to 30 minutes. Reserve the remaining marinade for later.

Heat 1 tablespoon (15 g) of the coconut oil in a large pan. Add the marinated chicken slices in a single layer and cook over high heat until lightly browned, 1 to 2 minutes. Work in batches if necessary: do not overfill the pan. Flip them over and cook for 1 to 2 minutes more, until crisped up. When done, transfer to a bowl, including the juices, and set aside.

Grease the pan with the remaining 2 tablespoons (30 g) coconut oil, and heat over high heat. Add the dried chiles and the blanched almonds. Cook for about a minute, until fragrant, stirring frequently. Add the celery and bell peppers to the pan. Cook for 1 to 2 minutes, while stirring and tossing. Add the ginger and garlic, and cook for another minute.

Add the chicken back to the pan. Stir in the remaining marinade and cook for 1 more minute, stirring frequently. Add the spring onions, stir, and remove from the heat. Serve with cauli-rice.

NUTRITION FACTS PER SERVING (EXCLUDES CAULI-RICE): Total carbs: 11 g | Fiber: 4.5 g | Net carbs: 6.5 g | Protein: 35.4 g | Fat: 38.2 g | Calories: 530 kcal
MACRONUTRIENT RATIO: Calories from carbs (5%), protein (28%), fat (67%)

Turkey Souvlaki with Supergreens Salad

4 SERVINGS
HANDS-ON TIME: 20 MINUTES
OVERALL TIME: 35 MINUTES +
MARINATING TIME

TURKEY SKEWERS

1½ lb (680 g) turkey breasts, cut into
   1½-inch (4-cm) pieces
½ cup (120 ml) extra-virgin olive oil
2 tablespoons (8 g/0.3 oz) chopped
   fresh mint
2 tablespoons (8 g/0.3 oz) chopped
   fresh parsley
1 tablespoon (4 g/0.1 oz) fresh thyme
3 tablespoons (45 ml) fresh lemon
   juice
1 teaspoon fresh lemon zest
1 medium (110 g/3.9 oz) white onion,
   sliced
2 cloves garlic, minced
½ teaspoon sea salt
¼ teaspoon black pepper

SUPERGREENS SALAD

¼ cup (60 ml) extra-virgin olive oil
1 teaspoon balsamic vinegar
1 tablespoon (15 ml) fresh lemon
   juice
1 pack (300 g/10.6 oz) mixed salad
   greens, such as lamb's lettuce,
   spinach, and arugula
2 medium (300 g/10.6 oz) avocados,
   pitted, peeled, and diced
2 medium (30 g/1.1 oz) spring onions,
   sliced
Optional: ½ cup (75 g/2.7 oz)
   crumbled feta cheese
Salt and pepper, to taste

Souvlaki is one of the most popular dishes in Greece. That's no accident: it's flavorful, easy to make, and requires minimum prep time. And these lemon- and herb-marinated turkey skewers are no exception! Serve them with a big bowl of supergreens salad dotted with creamy avocado and salty feta cheese.

TO MAKE THE TURKEY SKEWERS: Place the turkey chunks in a bowl. Add all the remaining ingredients. Stir to cover the meat in the marinade. Cover with plastic wrap, and refrigerate for at least 2 hours or for up to 24 hours.

When you're ready to cook, thread the turkey chunks onto skewers, about 4 per skewer. (You should end up with a total of 8 skewers.) Preheat the oven to 480°F (250°C, or gas mark 9) or, ideally, broil at 480°F (250°C). Transfer to the oven and cook for 10 to 15 minutes. Turn the skewers over halfway through the cooking process. Remove the skewers from the oven and let cool before transferring to a serving plate. Alternatively, pan-fry the skewers over medium-high heat on a hot griddle pan until browned on all sides and cooked through, 8 to 10 minutes.

TO PREPARE THE SALAD: Place the olive oil, balsamic vinegar, and lemon juice into a jar. Close with a lid and shake until the dressing is well combined. Place the greens into a large salad bowl. Add the avocado, spring onions, and feta cheese, if using. Toss with the prepared dressing, and season with salt and pepper to taste. Serve with the turkey skewers. The salad is best prepared fresh, but the skewers can be stored in the fridge for up to 4 days.

NUTRITION FACTS PER SERVING (2 SKEWERS + SALAD): Total carbs: 11.8 g | Fiber: 6.6 g | Net carbs: 5.2 g | Protein: 44.9 g | Fat: 40.3 g | Calories: 572 kcal
MACRONUTRIENT RATIO: Calories from carbs (4%), protein (32%), fat (64%)

Pork Schnitzel with Zesty Slaw

4 SERVINGS
HANDS-ON TIME: 25 MINUTES
OVERALL TIME: 25 MINUTES

SLAW

10.6 ounces (300 g) green or white cabbage, shredded

7.1 ounces (200 g) red cabbage, shredded

⅓ cup (75 g/2.6 oz) Mayonnaise (page 163)

2 tablespoons (30 ml) pickle juice or fresh lemon juice

2 medium (75 g/2.6 oz) pickles, grated

1 teaspoon Dijon mustard

½ teaspoon celery seeds

1 tablespoon (4 g/0.1 oz) chopped fresh dill

1 tablespoon (4 g/0.1 oz) chopped fresh parsley

Salt and pepper, to taste

SCHNITZEL

4 medium (600 g/1.3 lb) boneless pork chops

Salt and pepper, to taste

1 large pastured egg

1 tablespoon (15 ml) almond milk or water

½ cup (50 g/1.8 oz) almond flour

2.5 ounces (70 g) flax meal

2 tablespoons (30 g/1.1 oz) ghee or lard

Chopped fresh parsley

Lemon wedges

I grew up in the Czech Republic, where schnitzel is served during the holidays, so it always reminds me of our traditional Christmas feast. This healthier take on schnitzel omits the high-carb bread crumbs, replacing them with nutritious almond flour and flax meal, but otherwise, it's absolutely authentic! I love to serve it with a generous helping of colorful, zesty cabbage slaw.

TO MAKE THE SLAW: Place the green and red cabbage in a large bowl. In a small bowl, mix the mayonnaise, pickle juice, pickles, Dijon mustard, celery seeds, dill, and parsley. Pour this mixture over the cabbage, and combine well. Season with salt and pepper to taste, mix again, and set aside.

TO MAKE THE SCHNITZEL: Use a mallet to pound each pork chop to a thickness of ⅛ to ¼ inch (3 to 6 mm). Season with salt and pepper on both sides. Crack the egg into a bowl, add the almond milk, and whisk with a fork. In another bowl, mix the almond flour and flax meal. Dip each of the pork chops into the egg mixture, then dredge in the almond-and-flax mixture.

Heat a large pan greased with the ghee over medium heat. Once hot, cook the pork chops in a single layer for 3 to 4 minutes on each side, until golden brown. Serve warm with the prepared slaw, plus some fresh parsley and lemon wedges.

NOTE:
Make this recipe nut-free by substituting ½ cup (45 g/1.6 oz) grated Parmesan cheese for the almond flour.

NUTRITION FACTS PER SERVING (1 PORK CHOP + SLAW): Total carbs: 16.9 g | Fiber: 9.4 g | Net carbs: 7.5 g | Protein: 40.2 g | Fat: 48 g | Calories: 645 kcal
MACRONUTRIENT RATIO: Calories from carbs (5%), protein (26%), fat (69%)

Speedy Cauliflower-n-Cheese

4 SERVINGS
HANDS-ON TIME: 10 MINUTES
OVERALL TIME: 30 MINUTES

CAULIFLOWER BAKE

1 medium (600 g/1.3 lb) head
cauliflower

4 large (64 g/2.3 oz) slices cooked
bacon, crumbled

2 medium (30 g/1.1 oz) spring onions,
sliced

⅓ cup (30 g/1.1 oz) grated Parmesan
cheese

CHEESE SAUCE

¼ cup (56 g/2 oz) butter

½ cup (120 ml) heavy whipping
cream

½ cup (120 g/4.2 oz) cream cheese

½ teaspoon garlic powder

1½ cups (170 g/6 oz) grated Cheddar
cheese, divided

Cauliflower—an inexpensive keto kitchen staple—replaces the
"mac" in this luscious low-carb take on mac and cheese. A homemade, and truly finger-licking, cheese sauce smothers steamed
cauli, then the whole thing gets a sprinkling of crisp bacon, Parmesan, and sharp spring onions. Just try not to eat the whole thing
at once!

TO MAKE THE CAULIFLOWER BAKE: Preheat the oven to 450°F (230°C,
or gas mark 8). Cut the cauliflower into 1-inch (2.5-cm) pieces. Place
them in a steamer and cook for 8 to 10 minutes. Once cooked, remove
the lid and let the cauliflower cool for 5 minutes.

MEANWHILE, PREPARE THE CHEESE SAUCE: Place the butter and
cream in a small saucepan and heat gently. When hot, add the cream
cheese and garlic powder. Stir until melted and bring to a simmer.
Once you see bubbles, remove from the heat. Add 1 cup (113 g/4 oz) of
the Cheddar cheese, and mix until smooth and creamy.

Place the cooked cauliflower in a baking dish. Add the bacon,
spring onions, and prepared cheese sauce. Mix with a spoon until the
cauliflower is completely coated, and top with the grated Parmesan
and remaining ½ cup (57 g/2 oz) Cheddar cheese. Bake for 10 to
12 minutes, until the top is crispy and golden brown. Remove from
the oven and serve immediately, or let it cool and refrigerate for up
to 4 days.

NUTRITION FACTS PER SERVING: Total carbs: 10.9 g | Fiber: 3.3 g | Net carbs: 7.6 g | Protein: 23.9 g | Fat: 49.3 g |
Calories: 560 kcal
MACRONUTRIENT RATIO: Calories from carbs (5%), protein (17%), fat (78%)

Induction Carbonara

4 SERVINGS
HANDS-ON TIME: 20 MINUTES
OVERALL TIME: 30 MINUTES

2 packs (400 g/14.1 oz) shirataki noodles
2 small (300 g/10.6 oz) zucchini
Sea salt and black pepper, to taste
1 teaspoon ghee
4 egg yolks
1 cup (240 ml) heavy whipping cream
8 large (240 g/8.5 oz) slices bacon, chopped
½ cup (45 g/1.6 oz) grated Parmesan cheese
½ cup (8 g/0.3 oz) basil leaves

Induction is the initial phase of the ketogenic diet. It can be a difficult time, especially if you're suffering from keto flu and fighting cravings. If it's pasta you miss the most, go for this keto version of pasta carbonara. Made with zucchini and shirataki noodles, it won't kick you out of ketosis, but it's super filling and will knock those pasta cravings right out of the park.

Wash the shirataki noodles thoroughly and boil them in a pot in water to cover for 2 to 3 minutes. Drain well. Place the noodles in a hot dry pan and fry over medium-high heat for about 10 minutes, tossing the noodles as they cook. Set aside.

Use a julienne peeler or spiralizer to turn the zucchini into "noodles." Chop the cores and add them to the zucchini noodles. Sprinkle the zucchini noodles with salt and let them sit for 10 minutes, then use a paper towel to pat them dry. Pan-fry the noodles with a little ghee in a skillet over medium heat for 2 to 5 minutes, then set aside.

In a small bowl, combine the egg yolks with the cream and set aside.

Place the bacon pieces in a large heatproof casserole dish. Add ½ cup (120 ml) water. Cook over medium-high heat until the water starts to boil. Reduce the heat to medium, and cook until the water evaporates and the bacon fat is rendered. Reduce the heat to low and cook until the bacon is lightly browned and crispy.

Add the prepared shirataki noodles, and toss through with the bacon. Slowly start pouring in the cream–egg yolk mixture, stirring constantly, until it thickens. Add the spiralized zucchini and cook for 2 to 3 minutes. Finally, add the Parmesan and basil (chopped or whole), and season with salt and pepper, if needed. Eat immediately, or let it cool and refrigerate for up to 2 days.

NUTRITION FACTS PER SERVING: Total carbs: 7.9 g | Fiber: 2.2 g | Net carbs: 5.7 g | Protein: 17.1 g | Fat: 45.7 g | Calories: 505 kcal
MACRONUTRIENT RATIO: Calories from carbs (5%), protein (14%), fat (81%)

Pork Carnitas (a.k.a. Mexican Pulled Pork)

8 TO 10 SERVINGS
HANDS-ON TIME: 20 MINUTES
OVERALL TIME: 6 HOURS 20 MINUTES

2 teaspoons ground cumin

1 tablespoon (3 g/0.1 oz) dried oregano, preferably Mexican

1 tablespoon (17 g/0.6 oz) salt

1 teaspoon ground black pepper

4.4 pounds (2 kg) bone-in pork shoulder, or 3.5 pounds (1.6 kg) boneless pork shoulder

1 medium (110 g/3.9 oz) white onion, chopped

1 medium (14 g/0.5 oz) jalapeño pepper, sliced, seeds and membranes removed

4 cloves garlic, minced

Peel and juice of 1 small (100 g/ 3.5 oz) orange

Juice of 1 lime

¼ cup (60 ml) water

Optional: ¼ cup (55 g/1.9 oz) ghee or lard if using pork shoulder without under-skin fat layer

There's almost nothing as versatile (and delicious!) as slow-cooked Mexican-style pulled pork. And it's so easy to make: just rub Mexican spices over a pork shoulder and pop it into your slow cooker with citrus juices, onion, and jalapeño. A few hours later, it's ready to serve. Use Pork Carnitas to stuff a Keto Tortilla (page 11) for a quick dinner.

Preheat your slow cooker to high. Combine the cumin, oregano, salt, and pepper in a small bowl. Rinse and dry the pork shoulder. Using a sharp knife, remove the skin and leave the fatty part on the pork shoulder (reserve the skin for making Bone Broth, page 160). Rub the prepared spices all over the pork shoulder and place it in the slow cooker with the onion, jalapeño, and garlic. Pour the orange and lime juices over the pork shoulder, and add the orange peel and water. Cover and cook for 6 hours.

When done, remove the meat from the slow cooker and set aside to cool slightly before shredding it into pieces with two forks. Discard the orange peel. Using a ladle, skim off the fat from the juices in the slow cooker and keep it aside in a bowl: you'll use the fat to fry your carnitas. Reserve the cooking juices in another bowl. If the juices come to more than 2 cups (475 ml), pour them into a saucepan and cook until reduced.

Heat a pan greased with some of the reserved fat (alternatively, use ghee or lard) over medium-high heat. Place the shredded pork into the pan and press down. Cook for a few minutes, until crisped up, and place on a serving plate. Pour over some of the cooking juices and serve. You can store the meat in the fridge for up to 5 days and reheat in a pan or in the oven as needed. To freeze, store in manageable batches for up to 6 months.

NUTRITION FACTS PER SERVING (ABOUT 5.3 OZ/150 G COOKED MEAT): Total carbs: 4.4 g | Fiber: 1 g | Net carbs: 3.4 g | Protein: 34.9 g | Fat: 36.2 g | Calories: 490 kcal
MACRONUTRIENT RATIO: Calories from carbs (3%), protein (29%), fat (68%)

Pork Pot Roast with Vegetables

8 SERVINGS
HANDS-ON TIME: 15 MINUTES
OVERALL TIME: 4 HOURS + MARINATING

SPICE RUB

1 tablespoon (10 g/0.3 oz) garlic
   powder

1 tablespoon (7 g/0.2 oz) onion
   powder

1 tablespoon (5 g/0.2 oz) dried
   oregano

½ teaspoon fennel seeds

1½ teaspoons fine sea salt

1 teaspoon ground black pepper

POT ROAST

2.65 pounds (1.2 kg) pork shoulder,
   boneless

3 tablespoons (45 g/1.6 oz) ghee or
   lard, divided

2 bay leaves

1½ cups (360 ml) water, plus more if
   needed, divided

1 medium (110 g/3.9 oz) yellow
   onion, sliced

3 large (192 g/6.8 oz) celery stalks,
   sliced

4 medium (800 g/1.76 lb) turnips or
   kohlrabi, cut into 1-inch (2.5-cm)
   cubes, and/or halved baby turnips

10.6 ounces (300 g) dark-leaf kale,
   chopped and stems removed

When you think of pot roast, you probably think of beef, right? Well, when you apply the same process to a pork shoulder, the result is just as good. Massage the pork with a homemade spice rub, then slow-cook it in a Dutch oven with low-carb veggies until tender for the ideal winter weekend dinner.

TO MAKE THE RUB: Combine all the spices in a small bowl.

TO MAKE THE POT ROAST: Pat dry the pork using a paper towel and cover in the spice rub, pressing it all over. Place in plastic wrap, refrigerate, and let it marinate for 8 hours or up to 24 hours. (If you're short on time, marinating can be skipped.)

Preheat the oven to 350°F (175°C, or gas mark 4). Grease a large heavy-based saucepan or Dutch oven with half the ghee. Sear the marinated pork roast in the saucepan on all sides until the spice coating is golden brown, about 1 minute per side. Transfer to a deep casserole dish, and add the bay leaves and 1 cup (240 ml) of the water. Cover with a lid and cook for 3 hours.

In the meantime, grease a large heavy-based saucepan or Dutch oven with the remaining ghee. Add the onion and cook over medium-high heat for 5 to 8 minutes, until lightly browned. Add the celery, remaining ½ cup (120 ml) water, turnips, and kale. Cook for 1 to 2 minutes, until the kale is wilted. Remove from the heat and set aside.

After 3 hours of cooking, remove the casserole dish from the oven. Add the browned vegetables, cover with a lid, and put back in the oven. Cook, covered, for 1 hour, or until the vegetables are tender. When done, remove from the oven and set aside for 5 to 10 minutes. Discard the bay leaves and serve, or let it cool and refrigerate for up to 4 days or freeze for up to 3 months.

NUTRITION FACTS PER SERVING: Total carbs: 12.3 g | Fiber: 4.3 g | Net carbs: 8 g | Protein: 28.6 g | Fat: 33.4 g | Calories: 465 kcal
MACRONUTRIENT RATIO: Calories from carbs (7%), protein (26%), fat (67%)

Pizza Two Ways

1 PIZZA, 4 SERVINGS
HANDS-ON TIME: 15 MINUTES
OVERALL TIME: 1 HOUR 15 MINUTES

PIZZA CRUST

½ cup (50 g/1.8 oz) almond flour

⅓ packed cup plus 1 tablespoon
(2 oz/57 g) flax meal

2 tablespoons (15 g/0.5 oz) coconut
flour

1 tablespoon (4 g/0.1 oz) whole
psyllium husks or ½ tablespoons
(4 g/0.2 oz) psyllium husk powder

1 tablespoon (7 g/0.3 oz) ground chia
seeds

½ teaspoon sea salt

½ cup (120 ml) lukewarm water, plus
1 to 2 tablespoons (15 to 30 ml)
more if needed

¼ cup (22 g/0.8 oz) grated Parmesan
cheese

¼ cup (60 g) Marinara Sauce
(page 166)

**Choose one of the following
toppings:**

PEPPERONI PIZZA

1½ cups (170 g/6 oz) shredded
mozzarella cheese

28 small (57 g/2 oz) slices pepperoni

1 tablespoon (15 ml) extra-virgin
olive oil

¼ cup (15 g/0.5 oz) whole basil
leaves

One of the best things about this keto pizza is its dough. It's so versatile: I use it to make several different keto recipes, including tortillas, nachos, breadsticks, and even taco shells. Create your own version by topping it with your favorite low-carb ingredients: swap pesto for the Marinara Sauce (page 166), for instance, or top with eggs for a vegetarian option.

TO MAKE THE PIZZA CRUST: Mix all the dry ingredients in a bowl. Add the water, and combine well using your hands. If the mixture is too dry, add a splash more water. Leave to rest for 15 to 20 minutes. Meanwhile, preheat the oven to 400°F (200°C, or gas mark 6).

Place the dough between two pieces of baking paper and roll out until the dough is very thin, about ⅛ inch (3 mm) thick. Use your fingers to roll up the edges slightly, creating a rim to hold the filling. Sprinkle the crust with the Parmesan. Place the pizza crust on a baking sheet lined with parchment paper. Bake for 12 to 15 minutes, or until crispy and firm.

Spread the marinara sauce over the crust. Choose the topping you would like to use.

TO MAKE THE PEPPERONI PIZZA: Top the baked and sauced crust with the mozzarella and pepperoni slices (two slices at a time, one on top of the other—the finished pizza will look prettier this way!). Return to the oven and bake for another 12 to 15 minutes, or until the cheese is melted and the pepperoni is crisped up. Slice into 8 parts, drizzle the olive oil, and top with the chopped basil.

TO MAKE THE PROSCIUTTO & GOAT CHEESE PIZZA: Top the baked and sauced crust with the shredded mozzarella, prosciutto, and goat cheese. Add the onion and olives. Drizzle with 1 tablespoon (15 ml) of the olive oil. Return to the oven and bake for another 12 to 15 minutes, or until the cheese is melted and the prosciutto is crisped up. Slice into

NUTRITION FACTS PER SERVING (¼ PIZZA PEPPERONI/PROSCIUTTO & GOAT'S CHEESE): Total carbs: 12.5/13.1 g |
Fiber: 7.4/7.8 g | Net carbs: 5.1/5.3 g | Protein: 21.8/23.9 g | Fat: 35.6/37.2 g | Calories: 446/471 kcal
MACRONUTRIENT RATIO: Calories from carbs (5/5%), protein (20/21%), fat (75/74%)

PROSCIUTTO & GOAT CHEESE PIZZA

1 cup (113 g/4 oz) shredded mozzarella cheese

6 slices (90 g/3.2 oz) prosciutto di Parma

2 ounces (57 g) crumbled soft goat cheese

1 small (30 g/1.1 oz) red onion, sliced

8 pitted (25 g/0.9 oz) black or green olives, sliced

2 tablespoons (30 ml) extra-virgin olive oil, divided

1 cup (10 g/0.4 oz) arugula

8 parts, drizzle with the remaining 1 tablespoon (15 ml) olive oil, and top with the fresh arugula.

The pizza tastes best when eaten immediately, but can be stored in the fridge for up to 3 days and reheated in the oven.

NOTE:
To add extra shine to your pizza crust, you can brush the edges of the pizza with egg wash (1 egg yolk mixed with 1 to 2 teaspoons of water).

Healthy Deconstructed Hamburgers

4 SERVINGS
HANDS-ON TIME: 15 MINUTES
OVERALL TIME: 20 MINUTES

BURGERS

1.1 pounds (500 g) ground beef
Salt and pepper, to taste
1 tablespoon (15 g/0.5 oz) ghee or lard
Optional: 3 ounces (85 g) cheese of your choice (Cheddar, provolone, etc.)

BURGER SAUCE

¼ cup (55 g/1.9 oz) Mayonnaise (page 163)
1 tablespoon (15 g) sugar-free ketchup or tomato paste
1 teaspoon Dijon mustard
1 tablespoon (15 ml) fresh lemon juice
1 tablespoon (20 g/0.7 oz) grated pickle
Salt and pepper, to taste

TOPPINGS

1 large (600 g/1.3 lb) head iceberg lettuce
2 large (300 g/10.6 oz) tomatoes, sliced
8 small (200 g/7.1 oz) pickles, sliced

One of the perks of following a keto lifestyle is that burgers are actually good for you (as long as you skip the high-carb bun, that is). Here, perfectly cooked burgers get topped with homemade (highly addictive!) burger sauce, plus all of your favorite toppings, for a simple weeknight treat that's a real kid-pleaser.

TO MAKE THE BURGERS: Gently divide the ground meat into 4 equal parts. Use your hands to shape each piece into a loose burger, about 4 inches (10 cm) in diameter. (Do not squeeze or pack the meat too tightly, or the burgers will lose their juiciness as they are cooked.) Season with salt and pepper on each side.

Heat a large pan greased with the ghee over high heat. Use a spatula to transfer the burgers to the hot pan. Cook for 3 minutes, then flip over with the spatula, and cook for an additional 2 to 3 minutes. If using cheese, place it on top of the burgers for the last minute of the cooking process. Set aside.

TO MAKE THE BURGER SAUCE: Mix the mayonnaise, ketchup, Dijon mustard, lemon juice, and pickle in a bowl. Season with salt and pepper to taste.

TO ASSEMBLE THE TOPPINGS: Tear off the lettuce leaves (allow about ¼ head per person) and place in serving bowls. Top with the burger and serve with the tomatoes, pickles, and prepared burger sauce.

NOTE:
Pile on the extras! Add any low-carb topping you like, such as sliced avocado, pickled onions, jalapeño peppers, fresh tomato salsa, or kimchi.

NUTRITION FACTS PER SERVING (1 BURGER + 2 TABLESPOONS/30 G/1 OZ BURGER SAUCE + VEGETABLES):
Total carbs: 9.4 g | Fiber: 3.4 g | Net carbs: 6 g | Protein: 24.1 g | Fat: 40.7 g | Calories: 497 kcal
MACRONUTRIENT RATIO: Calories from carbs (5%), protein (20%), fat (75%)

Bacon-Wrapped Chorizo Meatloaf with Caramelized Cauliflower

6 SERVINGS
HANDS-ON TIME: 30 MINUTES
OVERALL TIME: 1 HOUR 30 MINUTES

MEATLOAF

1 pound (450 g) ground beef

½ pound (280 g) Mexican chorizo sausage

2 teaspoons onion powder

2 cloves garlic, minced

1 large pastured egg

1 teaspoon dried oregano

4 tablespoons (28 g/1 oz) flax meal

14 slices (300 g/10.6 oz) bacon

CAULIFLOWER

1 large (800 g/1.3 lb) cauliflower, sliced

1 medium (100 g/3.5 oz) red onion, sliced

6 cloves garlic, peeled

Few sprigs of fresh thyme

¼ cup (60 ml) melted ghee or duck fat

Salt and pepper, to taste

If you or your kids are convinced meatloaf is boring, I'm here to change your mind! This recipe uses both ground beef and chorizo sausage, so it has plenty of personality. Then it's wrapped in a "net" of bacon for extra flavor and crunch, and served with crisp caramelized cauliflower.

Preheat the oven to 375°F (190°C, or gas mark 5).

TO MAKE THE MEATLOAF: Combine all of the ingredients, except the bacon, in a bowl.

Next, prepare the "bacon net." Lay 6 slices of bacon on a chopping board (be sure to use streaky, thin-cut bacon, not Canadian-style bacon). Then weave the remaining 8 slices of bacon over and under the 6 slices to create a bacon net. (Search "bacon net" on the Internet for video tutorials!) Using your hands, shape the ground meat mixture into a meatloaf, about 4 x 10 inches (10 x 26 cm). Place the meatloaf on the side of the bacon net and roll it to wrap the net tightly around the meatloaf. Transfer it into the bacon net so that the longer side of the net is used to wrap around the meatloaf (not alongside the meatloaf). Place seam-side down in a baking dish lined with parchment paper. Transfer to the oven and bake for 1 hour.

TO MAKE THE CAULIFLOWER: Slice the cauliflower into about ½-inch-thick (1-cm) pieces. Lay the slices in a single layer on top of a baking sheet lined with parchment paper (you may need 2 trays to do this). Add the red onion, whole garlic cloves, and thyme. Drizzle with the melted ghee, and season with salt and pepper to taste. Place in the oven with the meatloaf, and bake for 45 to 50 minutes. Stir once or twice to prevent burning.

When done, remove the meatloaf and the cauliflower from the oven. Let both rest for 5 minutes. Slice the meatloaf and serve with the caramelized cauliflower. To store, refrigerate for up to 4 days.

NUTRITION FACTS PER SERVING (2 SLICES MEATLOAF + CAULIFLOWER): Total carbs: 13 g | Fiber: 5.1 g | Net carbs: 7.9 g | Protein: 32.2 g | Fat: 49.1 g | Calories: 620 kcal
MACRONUTRIENT RATIO: Calories from carbs (5%), protein (21%), fat (74%)

Beef Short Ribs with Coleslaw

6 SERVINGS
HANDS-ON TIME: 20 MINUTES
OVERALL TIME: 4 TO 5 HOURS + MARINATING

SPICE RUB

1 tablespoon (10 g/0.3 oz) garlic powder

1 tablespoon (7 g/0.2 oz) onion powder

2 teaspoons paprika

2 teaspoons fine sea salt

1 tablespoon (5 g/0.2 oz) dried oregano

¼ teaspoon cayenne pepper

SHORT RIBS

4 pounds (1.8 kg) beef short ribs (will yield about 50% meat)

½ cup (120 g/4.2 oz) Sweet & Sour BBQ Sauce (page 165), plus optionally more for serving

COLESLAW

1.3 pounds (600 g) sliced green or white cabbage, core removed

1 small (60 g/2.1 oz) red onion, sliced

½ cup (110 g/3.9 oz) Mayonnaise (page 163)

3 tablespoons (45 ml) fresh lemon juice

¼ cup (15 g/0.5 oz) chopped parsley or chives

½ teaspoon celery seeds

Salt and pepper, to taste

How do you make beef ribs that are fall-off-the-bone tender? Toss them into your slow cooker and forget about them for a few hours. Then brush them with barbecue sauce, pop them into the oven for 10 minutes, and serve them with a simple, naturally low-carb coleslaw.

Preheat the slow cooker to high and pour in ¼ cup (60 ml) water.

TO MAKE THE RUB: In a small bowl, mix all the spices and set aside.

TO MAKE THE SHORT RIBS: Pat dry the ribs using a paper towel and cover the short ribs in the spice rub, pressing it all over the ribs. Optionally, cover and marinate in the fridge for up to 8 hours. Transfer the ribs to the slow cooker and cook on high for 4 to 5 hours, until the meat is tender.

TO MAKE THE COLESLAW: Using your food processor's slicing blade, thinly slice the cabbage, and then place in a large mixing bowl. Add the red onion, mayonnaise, lemon juice, parsley, and celery seeds. Season with salt and pepper to taste, and mix well.

After 4 to 5 hours of cooking the ribs, using tongs, remove the ribs from the slow cooker and place on a baking sheet lined with heavy-duty parchment paper. Preheat the broiler. Brush the ribs with the BBQ sauce on all sides and place the ribs under the broiler. Cook on high for 8 to 10 minutes, turning halfway through.

Serve with the prepared coleslaw and more BBQ sauce, if desired. To store both the ribs and the coleslaw, refrigerate for up to 4 days. To freeze the ribs, shred the meat off the bones and freeze for up to 3 months (meat only).

NUTRITION FACTS PER SERVING: Total carbs: 11.7 g | Fiber: 4.1 g | Net carbs: 7.6 g | Protein: 28.5 g | Fat: 44.4 g | Calories: 547 kcal
MACRONUTRIENT RATIO: Calories from carbs (6%), protein (21%), fat (73%)

Beef Bourguignon

6 SERVINGS
HANDS-ON TIME: 20 MINUTES
OVERALL TIME: 5 TO 6 HOURS

BOUQUET GARNI

2 sprigs fresh parsley
2 sprigs fresh thyme
1 teaspoon peppercorns
3 whole cloves
3 bay leaves

STEW

2 pounds (900 g) beef chuck steak
   or brisket
Salt, to taste
3 tablespoons (45 g/1.6 oz) ghee or
   other healthy cooking fat, divided
1 medium (110 g/3.9 oz) white onion,
   chopped
3 cloves garlic, crushed
Optional: 1 medium (60 g/2.1 oz)
   carrot, sliced
1 bottle (750 ml) dry red wine, such
   as Burgundy, or 2 ¾ cups (656 ml)
   Bone Broth (page 160) plus 3 to
   6 tablespoons (45 to 90 ml) red
   wine vinegar
1 tablespoon (15 g/0.5 oz)
   unsweetened tomato paste
8 slices (240 g/8.5 oz) bacon, sliced
4 cups (300 g/10.6 oz) sliced white
   mushrooms
1 teaspoon fine sea salt, or to taste
Suggested side: Cauliflower Mash
   (page 132) or roasted green beans

If you've never made this classic French dish before, now's the time to start. It sounds complicated, but it's actually incredibly easy when you make it in a slow cooker. Serve it with Cauliflower Mash (page 132), roasted green beans, or steamed leafy greens. (Omit the carrot unless it fits within your daily carbohydrate limit.)

Preheat the slow cooker.

TO MAKE THE BOUQUET GARNI: Place all the herbs in a piece of cheesecloth and tie with unwaxed kitchen string.

TO MAKE THE STEW: Cut the beef into large chunks and season with salt. Heat a Dutch oven or a heavy-based pot greased with 2 table-spoons (30 g/1.1 oz) of the ghee. Fry the beef chunks in batches over medium-high heat until golden brown on all sides, about 5 minutes. Remove the chunks from the pot and place them in the slow cooker.

Add the onion, crushed garlic, and carrot (if using) to the pot where you browned the beef and lower the heat. Pour in the red wine and add the tomato paste. Bring to a boil and mix well with a spatula, scraping the caramelized cooking juices from the bottom of the pot. Pour into the slow cooker. Add the bouquet garni, cover with a lid, and cook on high for 4 to 5 hours. Remove the bouquet garni when the meat is cooked.

Grease a pan with the remaining 1 tablespoon (15 g/0.5 oz) ghee and crisp the bacon over medium heat for about 5 minutes. Add the mushrooms and cook for another 4 to 5 minutes, or until tender and browned. Remove from the heat and place in the slow cooker with the beef. Mix until well combined. To store, let it cool down, and refrigerate for up to 4 days or freeze for up to 3 months.

NUTRITION FACTS PER SERVING: Total carbs: 8.3 g | Fiber: 1.4 g | Net carbs: 6.9 g | Protein: 36.7 g | Fat: 45 g | Calories: 678 kcal
MACRONUTRIENT RATIO: Calories from carbs (5%), protein (25%), fat (70%)

Salisbury Steak with Quick Mash

4 SERVINGS
HANDS-ON TIME: 30 MINUTES
OVERALL TIME: 30 MINUTES

CAULIFLOWER MASH

1 medium (600 g/1.3 lb) cauliflower
2 tablespoons (30 ml) extra-virgin olive oil
Sea salt and black pepper, to taste

SALISBURY STEAK

1.1 pounds (500 g) ground beef
2 teaspoons onion powder
1 egg yolk
2 tablespoons (16 g/0.6 oz) coconut flour
½ teaspoon sea salt
¼ teaspoon black pepper
1 tablespoon (15 g/0.5 oz) ghee or duck fat

ONION GRAVY

3 tablespoons (45 g/1.6 oz) ghee or duck fat
1 large (150 g/5.3 oz) yellow onion, sliced
1 tablespoon (15 g/0.5 oz) unsweetened tomato paste
1 tablespoon (15 g/0.5 oz) Dijon mustard
1 tablespoon (15 ml) coconut aminos
1 cup (240 ml) Bone Broth (page 160) or chicken stock

Classic Salisbury steak bears a closer resemblance to hamburgers than it does to "real" steak, and it's traditionally served with fluffy mashed potato and lashings of onion gravy. This keto meal replaces the spuds with healthy cauliflower mash, and calls for a rich, homemade, tomato-laced gravy in place of the carb-laden, flour-rich variety.

TO MAKE THE CAULIFLOWER MASH: Cut the cauliflower into medium-size florets and place in a steamer. Cook for about 10 minutes. Remove from the heat, and place in a blender with the olive oil and season with salt and pepper to taste. Process until smooth, set aside, and keep warm.

TO MAKE THE SALISBURY STEAK: In a bowl, combine the beef, onion powder, egg yolk, coconut flour, salt, and pepper. Using your hands, create 4 patties (about 135 g/4.8 oz each) from the mixture. Grease a large skillet with the ghee. Once hot, add the burgers. Reduce the heat to medium and cook for about 3 minutes on each side. Do not flip the burgers too soon or they will stick to the pan. When done, set aside and keep warm.

TO MAKE THE GRAVY: Grease the pan in which you cooked the patties with the ghee. Add the onion and cook over medium-high heat for about 7 minutes, or until lightly browned and fragrant. Add the tomato paste, mustard, and coconut aminos, and cook for 1 minute. Pour in the bone broth, bring to a boil, then remove from the heat. Let the gravy cool for a few minutes, then pour into a blender and process until smooth.

Serve the cauliflower mash (about ¾ cup/160 g per serving) with the patties and pour over the gravy (about ¼ cup/60 ml per serving). Eat immediately, or store the patties and cauliflower mash in separate containers in the fridge for up to 4 days.

NUTRITION FACTS PER SERVING (1 BURGER + ¼ CUP/60 ML GRAVY + ¾ CUP/160 G MASH): Total carbs: 14.1 g | Fiber: 4.9 g | Net carbs: 9.2 g | Protein: 27.4 g | Fat: 49.7 g | Calories: 613 kcal
MACRONUTRIENT RATIO: Calories from carbs (6%), protein (18%), fat (76%)

Steak Fajitas with Avocado Salsa Verde

4 SERVINGS
HANDS-ON TIME: 25 MINUTES
OVERALL TIME: 25 MINUTES + MARINATING

MARINADE

2 cloves garlic, minced
½ cup (120 ml) extra-virgin olive oil
¼ cup (60 ml) fresh lime juice
1 teaspoon ground cumin
1 teaspoon chili powder
½ teaspoon red pepper flakes
1 teaspoon sea salt
¼ teaspoon black pepper

FAJITAS

1 medium (110 g/3.9 oz) yellow
    onion, sliced
1 medium (120 g/4.2 oz) red bell
    pepper, sliced
1 medium (120 g/4.2 oz) yellow bell
    pepper, sliced
1 medium (120 g/4.2 oz) green bell
    pepper, sliced
1.3 pounds (600 g) flank or skirt
    steak
2 tablespoons (30 g/1.1 oz) ghee or
    lard, divided
8 leaves (143 g/5 oz) lettuce
2 tablespoons (30 ml) extra-virgin
    olive oil

AVOCADO SALSA VERDE

½ cup (120 ml) (sugar-free) salsa
2 small (200 g/7.1 oz) avocados,
    pitted, peeled, and sliced

Speedy weekday dinners don't get better than these keto "fajitas." Bathe steak and low-carb vegetables in a spiced marinade, then toss them into a hot pan for a few minutes and serve them on top of lettuce leaves instead of high-carb tortillas, slathered with plenty of homemade avocado salsa verde.

TO MAKE THE MARINADE: Combine all the ingredients for the marinade in a bowl and set aside.

TO MAKE THE FAJITAS: Place the onion and peppers in one bowl, and the flank steak in another. Divide the marinade between the 2 bowls. Toss to combine until the meat and vegetables are thoroughly coated. Refrigerate for at least 1 hour or up to 24 hours.

When ready to cook, remove the steak from the marinade and pat dry. Place a large pan greased with 1 tablespoon (15 g) of the ghee over high heat. Once hot, cook the steak for 2 to 3 minutes on each side, depending on its thickness, until medium-rare. Do not overcook the steak. Remove from the pan and keep warm.

Grease the same pan with the remaining 1 tablespoon (15 g) ghee and place over high heat. Use a slotted spoon to add the vegetables to the pan. Cook for 3 to 5 minutes, stirring occasionally. (The leftover vegetable marinade can be used for making another batch of vegetables.)

TO MAKE THE SALSA: Combine the salsa and avocado in a bowl and stir to mix.

When ready to serve, slice the meat thinly against the grain. (If you use sirloin or rib eye, you won't need to cut the meat as thinly as you would with flank or skirt steak.) Serve on top of lettuce leaves (2 per serving) and drizzle with ½ tablespoon (7 ml) of olive oil, plus a quarter of the pepper mixture and the avocado salsa verde. Refrigerate the steak and peppers for up to 4 days (reheat gently to avoid overcooking), and refrigerate the avocado salsa in an airtight container for up to 3 days.

NUTRITION FACTS PER SERVING: Total carbs: 16.1 g | Fiber: 7.2 g | Net carbs: 8.9 g | Protein: 35.1 g | Fat: 40 g | Calories: 560 kcal
MACRONUTRIENT RATIO: Calories from carbs (7%), protein (26%), fat (67%)

Shepherd's Pie

6 SERVINGS
HANDS-ON TIME: 20 MINUTES
OVERALL TIME: 1 HOUR 15 MINUTES

2.2 pounds (1 kg) ground lamb
1 small (70 g/2.5 oz) white onion
1 medium (80 g/2.8 oz) carrot
2 cloves garlic
1½ cups (150 g/5.3 oz) white
    mushrooms
2 cups (200 g/7.1 oz) green beans
½ cup (120 ml) Bone Broth (page
    160) or vegetable stock
1 tablespoon (15 ml) Worcestershire
    sauce
1 teaspoon salt
Freshly ground black pepper, to
    taste
2 tablespoons (16 g/0.6 oz) ground
    chia seeds
1 large (800 g/28.2 oz) cauliflower
2 tablespoons (30 g/1.1 oz) butter
    or ghee
2 tablespoons (6 g/0.2 oz) chopped
    chives or fresh parsley

This hearty casserole is traditional British comfort food at its finest. It usually includes a carb-heavy mashed-potato topping, but I've replaced potato with creamy cauliflower, so it's perfectly suited to a keto diet. Go ahead and dig in!

Heat a large pan and add the ground lamb. Brown on all sides, stirring frequently, until the fat is released and the meat is cooked through. Use a slotted spoon to transfer the lamb to a bowl and set aside. Keep the cooking fat in the pan.

Peel and finely dice the onion and carrot and then peel and crush the garlic. Wash and slice the mushrooms. Wash and trim the green beans and chop them into quarters. Place the onion and garlic in the pan where you cooked the lamb. Cook for about 2 minutes, or until translucent, stirring frequently. Add the carrot, mushrooms, and green beans. Cook for a few more minutes, until the carrot begins to soften.

Return the cooked lamb to the pan and add the bone broth and Worcestershire sauce. Season with salt and black pepper to taste and simmer over low heat for 20 to 25 minutes. Remove from the heat and add the ground chia seeds. Mix until well combined.

Meanwhile, preheat the oven to 400°F (200°C, or gas mark 6) and prepare the cauliflower mash. Wash the cauliflower and cut it into medium florets. Place it on a steaming rack in a steaming pot filled with about 2 inches (5 cm) of water and cook for about 10 minutes.

When done, transfer the cauliflower to a blender and pulse until smooth and creamy. Add the ghee, season with salt and black pepper, and pulse again. Set aside.

Spread the lamb mixture into a casserole dish. Top with the mashed cauliflower. Using the tines of a fork, create a decorative pattern on top. Bake for about 30 minutes, until the cauliflower is golden in color. Remove from the oven and let it cool slightly before serving. Top with chopped chives or parsley.

NUTRITION FACTS PER SERVING: Total carbs: 13.9 g | Fiber: 5.3 g | Net carbs: 8.6 g | Protein: 33.7 g | Fat: 40 g | Calories: 537 kcal
MACRONUTRIENT RATIO: Calories from carbs (6%), protein (26%), fat (68%)

Lamb Vindaloo

4 SERVINGS
HANDS-ON TIME: 20 MINUTES
OVERALL TIME: 1 HOUR 30 MINUTES

SPICES

1 teaspoon coriander seeds

1 teaspoon fennel seeds

1 teaspoon fenugreek seeds

2 whole cloves

¼ teaspoon whole black peppercorns

LAMB

1 small (70 g/2.5 oz) white onion

2 cloves garlic

1 to 2 small hot chile peppers

1 tablespoon (8 g/0.3 oz) grated ginger

1 bunch cilantro

1.7 pounds (800 g) boneless
lamb shoulder

2 tablespoons (30 g/1.1 oz) butter
or ghee

1 teaspoon ground turmeric

1 teaspoon salt

Freshly ground black pepper, to taste

1 small can (200 g/7.1 oz) diced
tomatoes

1 tablespoon (15 ml) balsamic vinegar

1½ cups (480 ml) water

Optional: 1 cup (230 g/8 oz) full-fat
yogurt or sour cream, for serving

Are you as much of a spice fiend as I am? (There's good reason to be: the capsaicin in chiles has a ton of health benefits. It may help with pain relief, promote weight loss, and even help prevent certain types of cancer.) If you love the hot stuff, you'll adore this low-carb lamb vindaloo. It tastes just like the legendary Indian takeout version, but it's far healthier. This dish is perfect over Cauliflower Rice (page 13).

TO TOAST THE SPICES: In a dry, hot pan, toast all of the spices for a few minutes, until golden. Be careful not to let them burn.

TO MAKE THE LAMB: Peel and finely dice the onion and peel and crush the garlic. Wash, halve, and deseed the chile pepper. Wash the cilantro, separate the stalks from the leaves, and finely chop the stalks. Keep the remaining leaves for garnish. Dice the lamb into medium pieces and set aside.

Grease a large heavy pot or Dutch oven with the ghee and add the sliced onion, garlic, chiles, ginger, and cilantro stalks. Cook over medium heat for about 5 minutes, or until the onion starts to brown.

Add the lamb, toasted spices, turmeric, salt, and black pepper. Mix well and let the meat brown on all sides. Add the tomatoes, balsamic vinegar, and water. Turn the heat down to medium-low, cover with a lid, and cook for about an hour, or until the meat is tender.

Check the pot every 20 minutes to ensure there is enough water and that the vindaloo isn't sticking to the bottom. When done, remove from the heat and let it sit for a few minutes. Season with more salt if needed and serve with yogurt, if desired.

NUTRITION FACTS PER SERVING: Total carbs: 7.1 g | Fiber: 1.8 g | Net carbs: 5.2 g | Protein: 37 g | Fat: 41.9 g | Calories: 559 kcal

MACRONUTRIENT RATIO: Calories from carbs (4%), protein (27%), fat (69%)

Moussaka

8 SERVINGS
HANDS-ON TIME: 25 MINUTES
OVERALL TIME: 8 HOURS

The advantage to slow cooking is that you can do most of the prep work in the morning, turn the slow cooker on, and your favorite Greek casserole will be ready to serve by dinner.

MOUSSAKA

1 medium (400 g/14.1 oz) rutabaga

2 medium (680 kg/1.5 lb) eggplants

1½ teaspoons fine sea salt, or to taste

2 tablespoons (30 g/1.1 oz) ghee or lard

1 small (70 g/2.5 oz) yellow onion, chopped

2 cloves garlic, minced

2.2 pounds (1 kg) ground lamb

3 tablespoons (12 g/0.4 oz) chopped fresh oregano or 1 tablespoon (4 g/0.1 oz) dried oregano

3 tablespoons (12 g/0.4 oz) chopped fresh mint or 1 tablespoon (4 g/0.1 oz) dried mint

1 teaspoon ground cinnamon

½ teaspoon ground cloves

1 bay leaf, crumbled

¼ teaspoon ground black pepper

2 tablespoons (30 g/1.1 oz) unsweetened tomato paste

1 cup (240 ml) dry red wine, or ¾ cup plus 2 tablespoons (210 ml) Bone Broth (page 160) and 1 to 2 tablespoons (15 to 30 ml) red wine vinegar

BÉCHAMEL SAUCE

1½ cups (360 ml) heavy whipping cream

4 egg yolks

¼ teaspoon ground nutmeg

1 bay leaf, crumbled

1½ cups (135 g/4.8 oz) grated Parmesan cheese, divided

Salt and pepper, to taste

TO MAKE THE MOUSSAKA: Preheat the slow cooker and grease with ghee. Peel the rutabaga, then cut it and the eggplants into ¼-inch (½-cm) slices. Season the eggplant and rutabaga slices with salt and set aside for 20 minutes. Pat dry any excess moisture off the eggplant.

Meanwhile, grease a large heavy-based saucepan with the ghee. Add the onion and cook over medium-high heat for 5 to 8 minutes, until lightly browned. Add the garlic and lamb and cook over medium heat until browned on all sides, about 5 minutes, stirring frequently. Add the oregano, mint, cinnamon, cloves, bay leaf, black pepper, tomato paste, and red wine. Cook for 5 to 8 minutes, or until the sauce is reduced by half. Season to taste and set aside.

To assemble, place a layer of the rutabaga on the bottom of the slow cooker. Add a layer of eggplant (about a third of the amount) and half of the meat mixture. Add another third of rutabaga-eggplant and the remaining meat mixture. Top with the remaining rutabaga-eggplant. Cover with a lid and cook on low for 8 hours.

TO MAKE THE BÉCHAMEL SAUCE: In a saucepan, mix the cream, egg yolks, nutmeg, and crumbled bay leaf. Cook over medium-low heat, stirring constantly, until it starts to thicken. Take off the heat and mix in 1 cup (90 g/3.2 oz) of the grated Parmesan cheese. After 6 hours of cooking the moussaka, pour in the béchamel sauce. Sprinkle with the remaining ½ cup (45 g) Parmesan cheese, cover with the lid, and cook for another 2 hours.

Optionally, you can crisp the moussaka in the oven at 400°F (200°C, or gas mark 6) for 5 to 8 minutes, or until the top is golden brown. Serve immediately, or let it cool and refrigerate for up to 4 days or freeze for up to 3 months.

NUTRITION FACTS PER SERVING: Total carbs: 14.7 g | Fiber: 4.7 g | Net carbs: 10 g | Protein: 31.4 g | Fat: 52.8 g | Calories: 685 kcal
MACRONUTRIENT RATIO: Calories from carbs (6%), protein (20%), fat (74%)

Cheese-Stuffed Greek Bifteki

8 SERVINGS
HANDS-ON TIME: 35 MINUTES
OVERALL TIME: 55 MINUTES

BIFTEKI

2 pounds (900 g) ground lamb or beef

1 small (60 g/2.1 oz) red onion, minced

2 cloves garlic, crushed

1 large egg, white only, yolk reserved

1 large egg

2 tablespoons (8 g/0.3 oz) chopped fresh parsley

1 teaspoon dried oregano

2 tablespoons (30 ml) white wine vinegar

¾ teaspoon sea salt

½ teaspoon black pepper

⅓ cup (40 g/1.4 oz) coconut flour

1 tablespoon (15 ml) melted ghee or duck fat

BIFTEKI FILLING

1 cup (240 g/8.5 oz) cream cheese

1 egg yolk (reserved from the bifteki)

2 tablespoons (8 g/0.3 oz) chopped fresh parsley

1 teaspoon dried oregano

½ cup (75 g/2.6 oz) crumbled feta

GREEK-STYLE SALAD

½ cup (120 ml) extra-virgin olive oil

2 tablespoons (30 ml) fresh lemon juice

1 clove garlic, crushed

1.3 pounds (600 g) green beans, trimmed

2 cups (300 g/10.6 oz) halved cherry tomatoes

1 small (60 g/2.1 oz) red onion, sliced

1 cup (150 g/5.3 oz) crumbled feta

1 teaspoon each dried oregano and mint

¼ cup (34 g/1.2 oz) capers or olives

Bifteki are oval-shaped, cheese-stuff meat patties that are flavored with fresh herbs, and in Athens, they're a popular street food. After I fell in love with them in Greece, I just had to recreate them at home. And these are just like the real thing! For a complete meal, serve them with a big Greek salad.

TO MAKE THE BIFTEKI: Preheat the oven to 400°F (200°C, or gas mark 6). Place all the ingredients for the bifteki, except the ghee, in a bowl. Mix until well combined, then use your hands to form the mixture into 8 oval-shaped patties (about 150 g/5.3 oz each).

TO MAKE THE FILLING: Combine the cream cheese, egg yolk, parsley, oregano, and crumbled feta in a bowl. Spoon about 2 tablespoons (42 g/1.5 oz) of the cheese filling along the middle of the long side of each bifteki. Using your hands, fold each bifteki over gently without squeezing the cheese out. Place on a baking tray and brush each with the melted ghee. Transfer to the oven and bake for 30 to 35 minutes, until lightly browned on top and cooked through.

TO MAKE THE SALAD: Combine the olive oil, lemon juice, and crushed garlic in a small bowl and set aside. Bring a large pot filled with salted water to a boil. Add the green beans and cook for 3 to 4 minutes, until crisp-tender. Drain the beans, then immediately plunge them into ice water for 30 seconds. Drain and place into a bowl. Add the tomatoes, onion, crumbled feta, herbs, and capers. Drizzle with the dressing. Serve immediately alongside the bifteki. Refrigerate the cooked bifteki in an airtight container for up to 4 days, or freeze for up to 3 months. Refrigerate the salad in an airtight container for up to 2 days.

NUTRITION FACTS PER SERVING (1 BIFTEKI + SALAD): Total carbs: 13.1 g | Fiber: 4.3 g | Net carbs: 8.8 g | Protein: 29.9 g | Fat: 55.4 g | Calories: 652 kcal
MACRONUTRIENT RATIO: Calories from carbs (5%), protein (18%), fat (77%)

BROWNIE ALMOND CHEESECAKE BARS, PAGE 152

COOKIE DOUGH MOUSSE, PAGE 147

CHAPTER 7

SUGAR-FREE
Drinks and Desserts

ABOVE: SKILLET BERRY CRUMBLE, PAGE 146
CZECH BUTTER CAKE, PAGE 144

VANILLA KETO ICE
CREAM, PAGE 141

CHOCOLATE AND RASPBERRY
TRUFFLES, PAGE 142

VANILLA PANNA COTTA
WITH STRAWBERRY
COULIS, PAGE 149

FOR LOTS OF PEOPLE, THE HARDEST PART OF
starting a low-carb diet is giving up traditional sugary sweets.
Because weaning yourself off them can be tough, it's a good
idea to avoid all sweet treats when you're just beginning to
eat keto, even if they're sugar-free, as sweet-tasting foods of
all kinds can trigger cravings.

But once you've found your rhythm, there's nothing
wrong with enjoying dessert now and again! In the pages
that follow, you'll find recipes for all kinds of keto-friendly
desserts and drinks. If you're on a fat fast, try the Tiramisu
Ice Bombs on page 140 or the Almond Bliss Bars on page
143; they'll give you plenty of energy without kicking you
out of ketosis. Guests coming over for dinner? Make the
Cookie Dough Mousse, which is as ridiculously delicious
as it sounds, on page 147, or use your slow cooker to make
a quartet of Snickerdoodle Crème Brûlées (page 153)—
they're far easier to make than the traditional version! And
for a healthy, electrolyte-rich refresher, try the Raspberry
Electrolyte Limeade on page 155: it can help keep symptoms of keto flu at bay. The only question is, which recipe will
you make first?

ALMOND BLISS BARS, PAGE 143

Tiramisu Ice Bombs

12 ICE BOMBS
HANDS-ON TIME: 10 MINUTES
OVERALL TIME: 45 MINUTES + FREEZING

ICE BOMBS

1¼ cups (300 g/10.6 oz) full-fat
   mascarpone cheese or coconut
   cream
¼ cup (40 g/1.4 oz) powdered
   erythritol or Swerve
1 to 2 teaspoons sugar-free rum
   extract
¼ cup (60 ml) strong brewed regular
   or decaf coffee, chilled
Optional: Few drops liquid stevia,
   to taste

COATING (OR USE ANY OF THE HOMEMADE DARK CHOCOLATE RECIPES [PAGE 16])

2.5 ounces (70 g) extra-dark 90%
   chocolate
1 ounce (28 g) cacao butter

These frozen, chocolate-coated fat bombs taste just like my favorite Italian dessert—not least because they're made with mascarpone cheese, an essential ingredient in the traditional recipe. And with just five ingredients, they take absolutely zero effort to whip up. They're pretty filling, so try to stick to just one per sitting.

TO MAKE THE ICE BOMBS: In a food processor or with a mixer, combine the mascarpone or coconut cream, erythritol or Swerve, rum extract, and chilled coffee. Pulse until smooth and creamy. If you want a sweeter taste, add the stevia and pulse again.

Spoon about 2 tablespoons (35 g/1.2 oz) of the mixture into each of 12 small silicone muffin molds or candy molds, or use round cake pop molds for a round bomb shape. Freeze for about 2 hours, or until set.

TO MAKE THE COATING: Melt the dark chocolate and cacao butter in a double boiler or in a heatproof bowl placed over a small saucepan filled with 1 cup (240 ml) of water, over medium heat. Mix well. Cool the mixture before use. It should not be hot, but should still be liquid. If you are using any of the Homemade Dark Chocolate recipes on page 16, you may need as much as 4.6 to 4.9 ounces (130 to 140 g) to coat all the ice bombs.

Work in batches of 3 or 4 to prevent the ice bombs from melting. Gently pierce each frozen ice bomb with a toothpick or a fork. One at a time, hold the ice bomb over the melted chocolate and spoon the chocolate over it to coat completely. Turn the stick as you work until the coating is solidified. Place the coated ice bombs on a parchment-lined tray.

Freeze the coated pieces, in batches as you work, for at least 15 minutes to harden. Keep frozen for up to 3 months.

NUTRITION FACTS PER SERVING (1 ICE BOMB): Total carbs: 1.8 g | Fiber: 0.4 g | Net carbs: 1.4 g | Protein: 2 g | Fat: 14.5 g | Calories: 143 kcal
MACRONUTRIENT RATIO: Calories from carbs (4%), protein (6%), fat (90%)

Vanilla-Keto Ice Cream

YIELD: 8 SERVINGS/SCOOPS
HANDS-ON TIME: 10 MINUTES
OVERALL TIME: 45 MINUTES + FREEZING

1½ cups (360 g/12.7 oz) coconut
    cream
6 large egg yolks
2 large eggs
¼ cup (40 g/1.4 oz) powdered
    erythritol or Swerve
¼ cup (60 ml) MCT oil
2 teaspoons sugar-free vanilla
    extract or 1 teaspoon vanilla
    powder
Few drops liquid stevia, to taste
    (optional)

This low-carb ice cream is a scoopable fat bomb—and it's so ridiculously rich and creamy that you'll mistake it for frozen vanilla custard.

In a food processor, combine the coconut cream, egg yolks, eggs, erythritol or Swerve, MCT oil, and vanilla. Pulse until smooth and creamy. If you want a sweeter taste, add the stevia and pulse again.

    Pour the mixture into an ice cream maker and process according to the manufacturer's instructions. Once the ice cream is churned, freeze for about 30 minutes before serving. Keep frozen for up to 3 months.

NUTRITION FACTS PER SERVING (1 SCOOP [⅓ CUP/85 G/3 OZ]): Total carbs: 3.9 g | Fiber: 1 g | Net carbs: 2.9 g | Protein: 5.2 g | Fat: 27.1 g | Calories: 270 kcal
MACRONUTRIENT RATIO: Calories from carbs (4%), protein (8%), fat (88%)

Chocolate and Raspberry Truffles

16 TRUFFLES
HANDS-ON TIME: 20 MINUTES
OVERALL TIME: 20 MINUTES + CHILLING

TRUFFLES

1 cup (240 g/8.5 oz) full-fat mascarpone cheese or cream cheese, or coconut cream

¼ cup (60 ml) heavy whipping cream or coconut milk

¼ cup plus 1 tablespoon (50 g/1.8 oz) powdered erythritol or Swerve

½ cup (50 g/1.8 oz) almond flour

⅓ cup (30 g/1.1 oz) unsweetened cacao powder

Optional: Few drops liquid stevia, to taste

16 frozen raspberries (50 g/1.8 oz)

COATING (OR USE ANY OF THE HOMEMADE DARK CHOCOLATE RECIPES [PAGE 16])

2.8 ounces (80 g) extra-dark 90% chocolate

1.4 ounces (40 g) cacao butter

Mascarpone cheese, chocolate, and berries are a heavenly trio on their own, but when they're cloaked in a dark-chocolate coating, the result is absolutely irresistible. Serve these Chocolate and Raspberry Truffles to your guests after dinner alongside small cups of black coffee for the perfect finish to any meal.

TO MAKE THE TRUFFLES: In a bowl, mix together the mascarpone or cream cheese, coconut cream, and erythritol or Swerve. Add the almond flour and cacao powder and mix until well combined. If you want a sweeter taste, add the stevia and mix again.

Use a 1-ounce (30 g) scoop to portion 16 mounds of the mixture on a parchment-lined tray. Press a raspberry into the top of each. Freeze for at least 1 hour.

TO MAKE THE COATING: Melt the dark chocolate and cacao butter in a double boiler or in a heatproof bowl placed over a small saucepan filled with 1 cup (235 ml) of water, over medium heat. Remove from the heat and set aside to cool.

Gently pierce each frozen truffle with a toothpick or a fork. Working one at a time, hold each truffle over the melted dark chocolate and spoon the chocolate over it to coat completely. Turn the stick as you work until the coating is solidified. Place the coated truffles on a parchment-lined tray.

Refrigerate the coated truffles for at least 15 minutes to harden. Keep refrigerated for up to 5 days or freeze for up to 3 months.

NUTRITION FACTS PER SERVING (1 TRUFFLE): Total carbs: 3.3 g | Fiber: 1.3 g | Net carbs: 1.9 g | Protein: 2.5 g | Fat: 14 g | Calories: 140 kcal
MACRONUTRIENT RATIO: Calories from carbs (5%), protein (7%), fat (88%)

Almond Bliss Bars

10 BARS
HANDS-ON TIME: 20 MINUTES
OVERALL TIME: 20 MINUTES + CHILLING

Made with creamed coconut milk, shredded coconut, and coconut oil, these nut-studded Almond Bliss Bars make lovely after-dinner treats, but they're also excellent midafternoon or post-workout snacks. Coated in sugar-free dark chocolate, they're sweet, filling, full of good fats, and absolutely keto-friendly.

BARS

½ cup (120 g/4.2 oz) coconut cream

1½ cups (112 g/4 oz) unsweetened shredded coconut

¼ cup (55 g/1.9 oz) coconut oil, at room temperature

2 tablespoons (20 g/0.7 oz) powdered erythritol or Swerve

2 teaspoons sugar-free vanilla extract or 1 teaspoon vanilla powder

Pinch salt

Optional: Few drops liquid stevia, to taste

20 whole almonds (24 g/0.8 oz)

COATING (OR USE ANY OF THE HOMEMADE DARK CHOCOLATE RECIPES [PAGE 16])

2 ounces (56 g) extra-dark 90% chocolate

0.8 ounce (24 g) cacao butter

TO MAKE THE BARS: In a mixing bowl, stir together the coconut cream, shredded coconut, coconut oil, erythritol or Swerve, vanilla, and salt. If you want a sweeter taste, add the stevia and mix again. Use your hands to form the mixture into 10 small bars, about 1 ounce (32 g) each, and place them on a parchment-lined tray. Top each bar with 2 almonds. Freeze for about 30 minutes.

TO MAKE THE COATING: Melt the dark chocolate and cacao butter in a double boiler or in a heatproof bowl placed over a small saucepan filled with 1 cup (235 ml) of water, over medium heat. Remove from the heat, and set aside to cool.

Gently pierce each bar with a toothpick or a fork. Working one at a time, hold each bar over the melted dark chocolate and spoon the chocolate over it to coat completely. Turn the stick as you work until the coating is solidified. Place the coated bars on a parchment-lined tray and drizzle any remaining coating over them.

Refrigerate the coated bars for at least 15 minutes to harden. Keep refrigerated for up to 1 week or freeze for up to 3 months.

NUTRITION FACTS PER SERVING (1 BAR): Total carbs: 5.3 g | Fiber: 2.8 g | Net carbs: 2.5 g | Protein: 3.8 g | Fat: 17.8 g | Calories: 193 kcal
MACRONUTRIENT RATIO: Calories from carbs (5%), protein (8%), fat (87%)

Czech Butter Cake

16 SERVINGS
HANDS-ON TIME: 15 MINUTES
OVERALL TIME: 1 HOUR

4½ ounces (128 g) butter or ghee, melted, plus more for greasing
2 cups (200 g/7.1 oz) almond flour
½ cup (60 g/2.1 oz) coconut flour
¼ cup (25 g/0.9 oz) unflavored whey or other protein powder
1 teaspoon vanilla powder or 1 tablespoon (15 ml) sugar-free vanilla extract
1 teaspoon baking soda
¾ cup (150 g/5.3 oz) granulated erythritol or Swerve
6 large eggs
¼ teaspoon cream of tartar or ½ teaspoon lemon juice
1 cup (240 ml) lukewarm almond milk
¼ cup (60 ml) fresh lemon juice
1 tablespoon (6 g/0.2 oz) fresh lemon zest
¼ cup (22 g/0.8 oz) cacao powder
1 tablespoon (10 g/0.4 oz) powdered erythritol or Swerve

Whether you're eating keto or not, special occasions call for cake. Make this Czech Butter Cake—or *babovka* in Czech—the next time you're celebrating a birthday or holiday. Its taste and texture are a lot like pound cake, thanks to the addition of protein powder, but—unlike traditional pound cake—it's very low in carbs.

Grease a large Bundt cake tin with the butter. Preheat the oven to 300°F (150°C, or gas mark 2).

You will need three bowls: In the first bowl, combine the almond flour, coconut flour, protein powder, vanilla (unless using liquid extract), baking soda, and granulated erythritol. Separate the egg whites from the egg yolks. In the second bowl, use an electric mixer to beat the egg whites with the cream of tartar (or lemon juice) until soft peaks form. In the third bowl, whisk together the egg yolks, melted butter, almond milk, lemon juice, and lemon zest (and the vanilla, if using liquid extract).

To the bowl with the egg yolk mixture, slowly add the dry mixture. Stir until the batter is well combined. Mix in about one-third of the fluffy egg whites to make the batter lighter, then gently fold in the remaining egg whites.

Pour about two-thirds of the batter into the greased cake tin and use a spatula to spread evenly. Add the cacao powder to the remaining batter and mix. Spoon it into the tin and spread with a spatula. Transfer the tin to the oven and bake for about 45 minutes, until set.

Remove from the oven and place on a cooling rack. Let cool completely. Place a large plate on top of the cake, then flip over to release the cake. Dust with the powdered erythritol, slice, and serve. Store at room temperature, covered with a kitchen towel, for up to 3 days; refrigerate for up to 5 days; or freeze for up to 6 months.

NUTRITION FACTS PER SERVING (1 SLICE): Total carbs: 5.2 g | Fiber: 2.5 g | Net carbs: 2.7 g | Protein: 7.3 g | Fat: 15.8 g | Calories: 185 kcal
MACRONUTRIENT RATIO: Calories from carbs (6%), protein (16%), fat (78%)

Key Lime Pie in a Jar

4 SERVINGS
HANDS-ON TIME: 15 MINUTES
OVERALL TIME: 15 MINUTES

CRUST

⅓ cup (25 g/0.9 oz) unsweetened shredded coconut

⅓ cup (50 g/1.8 oz) almonds or sunflower seeds

1 tablespoon (15 g/0.5 oz) butter or coconut oil

¼ teaspoon salt

½ teaspoon vanilla powder or 1 to 2 teaspoons unsweetened vanilla extract

1 tablespoon (10 g/0.4 oz) erythritol or Swerve, or 3 to 5 drops liquid stevia

LIME LAYER

1 large (200 g/7.1 oz) avocado

1 cup (240 g/8.5 oz) mascarpone cheese or coconut cream

⅓ cup (80 ml) fresh Key lime juice

1 teaspoon finely grated Key lime zest

¼ cup (40 g/1.4 oz) powdered erythritol or Swerve, or 15 to 20 drops liquid stevia

Avocado is a trendy ingredient in vegan and low-carb desserts these days, and with good reason: its bland taste and creamy texture make it an ideal replacement for other types of fats. (Surprisingly, it's also a good partner for chocolate!) Here, it's combined with mascarpone or creamed coconut to make a quick, Key lime–flavored topping for a sweet, nut-based crust.

TO MAKE THE CRUST: Place the coconut in a hot, dry skillet and fry for 1 to 2 minutes, stirring frequently, until fragrant. Add the coconut, almonds, butter, salt, vanilla, and erythritol to a food processor. Process until the mixture is chopped as roughly or as finely as you like, then divide it among 4 jars.

TO MAKE THE LIME LAYER: Halve the avocado and remove the seed. Scoop the avocado flesh into a blender with the mascarpone cheese, lime juice, lime zest, and erythritol. Process until smooth. Place an equal amount of the mixture into each jar on top of the crusts. Serve immediately, or cover the jars with plastic wrap and store in the fridge for up to 3 days.

NUTRITION FACTS PER SERVING: Total carbs: 11.8 g | Fiber: 6 g | Net carbs: 5.8 g | Protein: 8.4 g | Fat: 38.4 g | Calories: 418 kcal
MACRONUTRIENT RATIO: Calories from carbs (6%), protein (8%), fat (86%)

Skillet Berry Crumble

6 SERVINGS
HANDS-ON TIME: 10 MINUTES
OVERALL TIME: 25 MINUTES

BERRY BASE

1 tablespoon (15 g/0.5 oz) ghee or coconut oil
2 cups (300 g/10.6 oz) mixed berries (raspberries, blackberries, strawberries, and/or blueberries), fresh or frozen
Optional: 5 to 10 drops liquid stevia

CRUMBLE

1 cup (140 g/5 oz) almonds
½ cup (55 g/1.9 oz) pecans
2 tablespoons (30 g/1 oz) butter or coconut oil
1 teaspoon ground cinnamon or vanilla powder
¼ teaspoon salt
Optional: 2 tablespoons (20 g/0.7 oz) erythritol or Swerve, or 5 to 10 drops liquid stevia

This one-skillet dessert is a great way to use up your stock of late-summer berries—but because frozen berries are available in supermarkets year-round, you don't have to wait for warm weather to enjoy it! It's topped with a sugar-free crumble made from almonds, pecans, and cinnamon, and it's divine with a side of crème fraîche or Greek yogurt.

Preheat the oven to 400°F (200°C, or gas mark 6).

TO MAKE THE BERRY BASE: Heat a medium-size skillet greased with the ghee over medium-high heat. Add the berries and cook for 3 to 5 minutes, until softened. Taste and add stevia if desired. Set aside.

TO MAKE THE CRUMBLE: Place the almonds and pecans (preferably soaked and dehydrated) into a food processor. Add the butter, cinnamon, salt, and erythritol (if using). Pulse for a few seconds until the mixture is chopped as roughly or as finely as you like.

Sprinkle the nut mixture on top of the berries and broil for about 10 minutes, until lightly browned and crisp on top. Transfer to a cooling rack and let cool for 5 minutes. Serve warm or cold with a dollop of mascarpone cheese, sour cream, full-fat yogurt, or coconut cream flavored with vanilla extract.

NOTE:
You can make this crumble with any kind of nuts (macadamia, walnuts, or hazelnuts), seeds (sunflower, hemp, or pumpkin), or even shredded unsweetened coconut.

NUTRITION FACTS PER SERVING: Total carbs: 10.8 g | Fiber: 5.3 g | Net carbs: 5.5 g | Protein: 6.4 g | Fat: 24.8 g | Calories: 275 kcal
MACRONUTRIENT RATIO: Calories from carbs (8%), protein (10%), fat (82%)

Cookie Dough Mousse

6 SERVINGS
HANDS-ON TIME: 5 MINUTES
OVERALL TIME: 5 MINUTES

1 package (250 g/8.8 oz) mascarpone cheese

1¼ cups (300 ml) heavy whipping cream

½ cup (125 g/4.4 oz) Toasted Nut Butter, at room temperature (page 169)

2 teaspoons fresh lemon zest

1 teaspoon vanilla bean powder or ground cinnamon

¼ cup (40 g/1.4 oz) powdered erythritol or Swerve

½ cup (90 g/3.2 oz) 90% dark chocolate chips (or at least 85% chocolate)

I came up with this recipe by accident when I was looking for a way to use up leftover nut butter. And it turned out so well that it quickly became a favorite in our house! This cookie dough mousse takes just five minutes and a handful of ingredients to make, and it's so pretty when it's served in small glass jars.

Place all of the ingredients except the chocolate chips in a bowl. Using an electric mixer, process until smooth and creamy. Mix in the chocolate chips (reserve some for topping). Divide the cookie dough mousse among six 4-ounce (112 g) jars, and top with the reserved chocolate chips. If you have time, place in the fridge for 2 hours before serving. Store in the fridge for up to 4 days.

NUTRITION FACTS PER SERVING: Total carbs: 9.4 g | Fiber: 3.4 g | Net carbs: 6 g | Protein: 7.4 g | Fat: 55.3 g | Calories: 552 kcal
MACRONUTRIENT RATIO: Calories from carbs (4%), protein (5%), fat (91%)

Chewy Pumpkin and Chocolate Chip Cookies

10 SERVINGS
HANDS-ON TIME: 10 MINUTES
OVERALL TIME: 25 MINUTES

1 cup (250 g/8.8 oz) almond butter
  or sunflower seed butter
1 large pastured egg
⅓ cup (65 g/2.3 oz) unsweetened
  pumpkin purée
1 tablespoon (8 g/0.3 oz) pumpkin
  pie spice mix
2 tablespoons (20 g/0.7 oz)
  erythritol or Swerve
Optional: 5 to 10 drops liquid stevia
¼ teaspoon salt
½ cup (90 g/3.2 oz) dark chocolate
  chips or roughly chopped
  chocolate (85% cacao or more)

Beat those midmorning sugar cravings! Here's how: skip the high-sugar treats that are always lurking in the office kitchen and treat yourself to one of these chewy, spicy, chocolaty cookies instead. There's no better match for a cup of coffee or tea.

Preheat the oven to 350°F (175°C, or gas mark 4). Place all the ingredients except the chocolate chips into a food processor. Pulse until smooth. Scoop the cookie dough into a bowl and add the chocolate chips. Mix well with a wooden spoon.

Line a baking sheet with parchment paper. Using a spoon or a cookie scoop, create 10 mounds of dough. Place them on the parchment-lined tray, and flatten each with a fork or spoon. Bake for 13 to 15 minutes, until lightly golden and cooked through. Transfer to a wire rack to cool. (The cookies will crisp up slightly as they cool.) Store in an airtight container for up to a week, or freeze for up to 3 months.

NUTRITION FACTS PER SERVING (1 COOKIE): Total carbs: 8.4 g | Fiber: 4.4 g | Net carbs: 4 g | Protein: 6.4 g | Fat: 17.1 g | Calories: 224 kcal
MACRONUTRIENT RATIO: Calories from carbs (8%), protein (13%), fat (79%)

Vanilla Panna Cotta with Strawberry Coulis

5 SERVINGS
HANDS-ON TIME: 20 MINUTES
OVERALL TIME: 3 TO 4 HOURS

PANNA COTTA

2½ cups (600 ml) heavy whipping cream or full-fat coconut milk
¼ cup (50 g/1.8 oz) granulated erythritol or Swerve, or 20 to 30 drops liquid stevia
½ teaspoon vanilla powder or 2 teaspoons unsweetened vanilla extract
1 tablespoon (11 g/4 oz) gelatin powder
¼ cup (60 ml) cold water

STRAWBERRY COULIS

2 cups (288 g/10.2 oz) fresh strawberries
1 tablespoon (15 ml) water
⅛ teaspoon vanilla powder or ½ teaspoon unsweetened vanilla extract
Optional: 1 tablespoon (10 g/0.4 oz) granulated erythritol or Swerve, or 3 to 5 drops liquid stevia

It's a question that's challenged philosophers for centuries: Vanilla or chocolate? That's a tough one, but if I had to pick just one, I'd go for vanilla—just so I could eat this silky-smooth vanilla panna cotta. And refreshing strawberry sauce, or coulis, is the perfect counterpoint to this classic high-fat treat.

TO MAKE THE PANNA COTTA: Place the cream, erythritol, and vanilla into a saucepan. Heat over medium heat, and stir until the sweetener has dissolved.

Sprinkle the gelatin powder over the cold water, and set aside to let it bloom. Once ready, pour and scrape the gelatin into the hot cream mixture. Mix well until all the gelatin has dissolved. Optionally, strain the mixture through a fine-mesh sieve to remove any vanilla seeds.

Pour into five 4-ounce (112 g) serving glasses and fill them about two-thirds full, leaving enough space for the strawberry coulis. Place in the fridge for 3 to 4 hours, or until set.

TO MAKE THE STRAWBERRY COULIS: Slice the strawberries and place them in a saucepan (optionally, keep 5 strawberries for topping). Add the water. Mix in the vanilla powder and add the erythritol, if using. Gently heat over medium-low heat until the strawberries have softened, about 5 minutes. Remove from the heat, and set aside to cool to room temperature.

When the panna cotta has set, evenly distribute the cooled strawberry coulis among the 5 jars. Finish with sliced strawberries, if using. Serve immediately or store in the fridge for up to 4 days.

NUTRITION FACTS PER SERVING: Total carbs: 8.1 g | Fiber: 1.1 g | Net carbs: 7 g | Protein: 4.5 g | Fat: 45.8 g | Calories: 469 kcal
MACRONUTRIENT RATIO: Calories from carbs (6%), protein (4%), fat (90%)

Boston Cream Pie

12 SERVINGS
HANDS-ON TIME: 35 MINUTES
OVERALL TIME: 2 HOURS

SPONGE BASE

¼ cup (30 g/1.1 oz) coconut flour

2 cups (200 g/7.1 oz) almond flour

¼ cup (25 g/0.9 oz) whey protein or egg white protein, vanilla or unflavored

1 teaspoon baking soda

2 teaspoons cream of tartar

¼ teaspoon salt

½ cup (80 g/2.8 oz) powdered erythritol or Swerve

¼ cup (56 g/2 oz) butter or coconut oil, softened

4 large eggs

1 vanilla bean or 1 teaspoon unsweetened vanilla extract

½ cup (120 ml) almond milk

15 to 20 drops liquid stevia

Boston cream pie is the ultimate treat. Is there anything more decadent than sponge cake stuffed with custard and coated in dark chocolate? Not if you ask me! This keto version takes a little extra time and effort, but a single bite will show you that all your work was worth it.

TO MAKE THE SPONGE BASE: Preheat the oven to 350°F (175°C, or gas mark 4). Line a cake pan with a removable bottom with parchment paper.

Sift the flours, protein powder, baking soda, cream of tartar, and salt into a bowl and mix until well combined.

In a separate bowl, beat together the erythritol and softened butter or coconut oil. Gradually add the eggs and beat until light and creamy. Cut the vanilla bean lengthwise and scrape the seeds into the mixture (or add the vanilla extract). Slowly pour in the almond milk, and while whisking, add the liquid stevia, then fold in the dry ingredients.

Pour the batter into the cake pan and transfer to the oven. Bake for 30 to 35 minutes, or until the top is golden brown and the inside is fluffy and firm.

TO MAKE THE VANILLA CREAM FILLING: Pour the cream and ¼ cup (60 ml) of the almond milk into a saucepan and gently bring to a boil over medium heat. Mix the remaining ¼ cup (60 ml) almond milk with the arrowroot powder and set aside.

In a separate bowl, beat together the egg yolks, powdered erythritol, liquid stevia, vanilla bean seeds or extract, and salt. Pour two ladlefuls, one at a time, of the hot cream into the beaten eggs, stirring constantly. Then, pour the egg mixture into the remaining hot cream and keep stirring to prevent the eggs from scrambling.

Cook and stir constantly until the filling starts to thicken. Then, add the arrowroot mixed with almond milk—you may need to stir it again before pouring it into the custard. Cook for another minute and

NUTRITION FACTS PER SERVING: Total carbs: 9 g | Fiber: 3.2 g | Net carbs: 5.8 g | Protein: 10.2 g | Fat: 35.4 g | Calories: 386 kcal
MACRONUTRIENT RATIO: Calories from carbs (6%), protein (11%), fat (83%)

VANILLA CREAM CUSTARD

1 cup (240 ml) heavy whipping
    cream or coconut milk
½ cup (120 ml) almond milk, divided
1 tablespoon (9 g/0.3 oz) arrowroot
    powder
4 large egg yolks
¼ cup (40 g/1.4 oz) powdered
    erythritol or Swerve
10 to 15 drops liquid stevia
1 vanilla bean or 1 teaspoon
    unsweetened vanilla extract
Pinch salt
¼ (56 g/2oz) butter or coconut oil

CHOCOLATE GANACHE

1 bar (100 g/3.5 oz) extra-dark
    chocolate (85% cacao or more)
2 tablespoons (30 g/1.1 oz) butter or
    coconut oil
1 vanilla bean or 1 teaspoon
    unsweetened vanilla extract
¼ cup (60 ml) heavy whipping cream
    or coconut milk

remove from the heat. Add the butter or coconut oil and mix until well combined. Cover the surface with plastic wrap, let it cool, and then refrigerate. Alternatively, place the bowl in ice water and stir until chilled.

TO MAKE THE CHOCOLATE GANACHE: When the cake is ready to be assembled, make the ganache. Break the chocolate into small pieces and place in a bowl with the butter or coconut oil and vanilla seeds or extract. Heat the cream in a small saucepan over medium heat and, when boiling, pour over the chocolate and butter. Mix until smooth and creamy. Leave to cool slightly before spreading on the cake.

Cut the cake horizontally through the middle and spread the vanilla cream filling over the bottom half. Place the other half on top and pour the ganache over it, allowing it to drip down the sides. Leave to set or refrigerate before cutting into slices.

NOTES:
- You can substitute coconut oil for butter or ghee in most recipes. However, when cool, coconut oil tends to be harder than butter: keep this in mind when using it to make frostings, glazes, and ganaches.
- Don't waste the egg whites! You can use them to make the Sourdough Keto Buns on page 10.

Brownie Almond Cheesecake Bars

13 SERVINGS
HANDS-ON TIME: 20 MINUTES
OVERALL TIME: 4 HOURS

CHEESECAKE LAYER

1 cup (240 g/8.5 oz) full-fat cream cheese, at room temperature

¼ cup (58 g/2 oz) full-fat sour cream

½ cup (125 g/4.4 oz) almond butter, softened

1 egg yolk

1 large egg

¼ cup (40 g/1.4 oz) powdered erythritol or Swerve

½ teaspoon ground cinnamon

1 teaspoon sugar-free almond extract

Optional: Few drops of liquid stevia

BROWNIE LAYER

3.5 ounces (100 g) dark chocolate (minimum 85% cacao)

4.4 ounces (125 g) butter or coconut oil, melted

3 large eggs

¾ cup (120 g/4.2 oz) powdered erythritol or Swerve

1 cup (100 g/3.5 oz) almond flour

½ cup (43 g/1.5 oz) cacao powder

¼ cup (32 g/1.1 oz) ground chia seeds

2 teaspoons gluten-free baking powder

¼ teaspoon fine sea salt

Slow cookers are usually used to make stews and other savory dishes, right? Well, yes, but you can also use yours to "bake" luscious desserts like this one, in which rich, nutty cheesecake partners up with fudgy chocolate brownies. It's hard to believe, but it's true: they're actually sugar-free! Serve them at your next barbecue or picnic.

TO MAKE THE CHEESECAKE LAYER: Line the slow cooker with heavy-duty parchment paper. Preheat the cooker to low. Place all the cheesecake ingredients in a mixing bowl and set aside.

TO MAKE THE BROWNIE LAYER: Break the chocolate into pieces and add to a heatproof bowl with the butter. Place over a pan filled with simmering water and make sure the water doesn't touch the bowl: only the steam should heat the bowl. Slowly melt while stirring. When most of the chocolate is melted, remove the pan from the burner and let the mixture continue to melt. Set aside.

Place the eggs and powdered erythritol in another bowl and whisk until well combined. Beat in the chocolate mixture and gently fold in the almond flour, cacao powder, ground chia seeds, baking powder, and salt, and process well.

Pour the brownie batter into the slow cooker and spread evenly. Top with the prepared cheesecake mixture. Cover and cook on low for 3 to 4 hours. When done, remove the lid and let cool. Once cooled, grab the parchment paper to remove the cake from the slow cooker, and slice. To store, place in an airtight container. Refrigerate for up to 5 days or freeze for up to 6 months.

NUTRITION FACTS PER SERVING: Total carbs: 10 g | Fiber: 4.6 g | Net carbs: 5.4 g | Protein: 9 g | Fat: 29.3 g | Calories: 323 kcal
MACRONUTRIENT RATIO: Calories from carbs (7%), protein (11%), fat (82%)

Snickerdoodle Crème Brûlée

4 SERVINGS
HANDS-ON TIME: 10 MINUTES
OVERALL TIME: 2 TO 3 HOURS + CHILLING

2 cups (480 ml) coconut milk or
  heavy whipping cream
5 egg yolks
¼ cup (40 g/1.4 oz) powdered
  erythritol or Swerve, plus
  4 teaspoons granulated erythritol
  or Swerve for topping
1 teaspoon ground cinnamon
½ teaspoon vanilla powder or
  2 teaspoons sugar-free vanilla
  extract
Pinch salt

Think crème brûlée is too complicated to make at home? Well, making a sugar-free version in your slow cooker couldn't be simpler. If you've got ten minutes and six basic ingredients on hand, you can create creamy, cinnamon-laced custards that are a stunning finale to any meal.

Preheat the slow cooker and fill it with 1 cup (240 ml) of boiling water. Place a trivet inside the slow cooker. Combine all the ingredients, apart from the 4 teaspoons of erythritol, in a bowl using a whisk. Pour the mixture into 4 ramekins and place them on top of the trivet, cover the slow cooker with a lid, and cook on low for 2 to 3 hours, until the custard is set. Remove the lid and let the custards cool to room temperature. Cover each ramekin with plastic wrap. Refrigerate for at least 2 hours or overnight.

When ready to serve, sprinkle each one with 1 teaspoon of granulated erythritol or Swerve (see tip below). Place under a broiler set to high for 3 to 5 minutes to caramelize, or use a blowtorch.

NOTE:
You can use Swerve to make the caramelized topping. Although erythritol will create a hard shell, it will not brown. Swerve contains fructooligosaccharides, which will help the tops brown and create the sugar effect.

NUTRITION FACTS PER SERVING: Total carbs: 5 g | Fiber: 0.3 g | Net carbs: 4.7 g | Protein: 5.7 g | Fat: 29.8 g | Calories: 295 kcal
MACRONUTRIENT RATIO: Calories from carbs (6%), protein (7%), fat (87%)

Creamy Dark Hot Chocolate

1 SERVING
HANDS-ON TIME: 5 MINUTES
OVERALL TIME: 10 MINUTES

½ cup (120 ml) coconut milk or
heavy whipping cream
½ cup (120 ml) water or almond milk
2 cardamom pods, crushed
⅛ teaspoon ground cinnamon
¼ teaspoon sugar-free vanilla
extract or ⅛ teaspoon vanilla
powder
Pinch salt
2 tablespoons (20 g/0.7 oz)
granulated erythritol or Swerve
1 ounce (28 g) unsweetened
chocolate
1 tablespoon (15 ml) MCT oil or
coconut oil
Optional: Few drops liquid stevia,
to taste

This is the only hot chocolate recipe you'll ever need. Made with dark chocolate, coconut milk, vanilla, and spices, it's incredibly rich, but perfectly healthy. Add a pinch of cayenne if you like your hot chocolate that bit hotter, but don't skip the cardamom: somehow it manages to add extra depth and complexity to the dark chocolate.

In a small saucepan, combine the coconut milk or heavy cream, water or almond milk, cardamom, cinnamon, vanilla, salt, and erythritol or Swerve. Bring to a boil. When bubbles form on top, remove the mixture from the heat and let it sit for 5 minutes. Add the unsweetened chocolate and MCT oil and let it melt while stirring. If you want a sweeter taste, add the stevia and stir again.

Pour the chocolate mixture through a sieve into a blender and pulse for a few seconds until smooth and frothy. Serve hot!

NUTRITION FACTS PER SERVING: Total carbs: 11.6 g | Fiber: 4.2 g | Net carbs: 7.4 g | Protein: 6.3 g | Fat: 52.9 g |
Calories: 528 kcal
MACRONUTRIENT RATIO: Calories from carbs (5%), protein (5%), fat (90%)

Raspberry Electrolyte Limeade

6 CUPS (1.4 L)
HANDS-ON TIME: 5 MINUTES
OVERALL TIME: 20 MINUTES

2 cups (246 g/8.7 oz) raspberries, fresh or frozen

5 cups (1.2 L) still or sparkling water or hibiscus tea, divided

⅓ cup (53 g/1.9 oz) powdered erythritol or Swerve, or stevia to taste

½ cup (120 ml) fresh lime or lemon juice

2 tablespoons (12 g/0.4 oz) Natural Calm magnesium (see Note)

½ teaspoon food-grade potassium chloride (see Note)

¼ teaspoon sea salt

Lemon or lime slices

Fresh mint leaves, for serving

Optional: Ice cubes

This recipe is a fusion of two of my favorites: my own electrolyte drink and a raspberry lemonade adapted from fellow blogger Carolyn Ketchum over at AllDayIDreamAboutFood.com. It's a tasty—not to mention much healthier—alternative to electrolyte sports drinks. It's ideal for after workouts or during the initial phase of the ketogenic diet when keto flu symptoms are liable to strike.

Place the raspberries into a saucepan and add 1 cup (240 ml) of the water. Bring to a simmer to let the raspberries soften. Remove from the heat and set aside. Strain through a fine-mesh sieve into another saucepan. Use a large spoon to push the pulp through the sieve. Discard the seeds.

Add the erythritol and stir until dissolved. Add the lime juice, Natural Calm magnesium, potassium chloride, salt, and remaining 4 cups (960 ml) water. Stir again. Garnish with lemon or lime slices and fresh mint. Serve immediately over ice, if you like, or store in the fridge for 3 to 4 days.

NOTE:
For best results, and to avoid stomach distress, always drink Raspberry Electrolyte Limeade with meals, and do not consume more than 2 cups (480 ml) per day; ideally, start with 1 cup (240 ml) per day. Sweeteners can be omitted; use them to taste. If you can't find potassium chloride, you can use ¾ teaspoon of Morton Lite Salt and skip the sea salt.

NUTRITION FACTS PER SERVING (1 CUP/240 ML): Total carbs: 7 g | Fiber: 2.7 g | Net carbs: 4.3 g | Protein: 0.6 g | Fat: 0.3 g | Calories: 28 kcal
MACRONUTRIENT RATIO: Calories from carbs (78%), protein (10%), fat (12%)

Keto "Peanut" Butter Cups

8 SERVINGS
HANDS-ON TIME: 20 MINUTES
OVERALL TIME: 1 HOUR

TOASTED ALMOND-CASHEW BUTTER

1 cup (150 g/5.3 oz) almonds, blanched or whole

⅓ cup (50 g/1.8 oz) cashews

¼ cup (60 ml) almond oil or macadamia nut oil

⅛ teaspoon sea salt

Optional: 2 tablespoons (20 g/0.7 oz) powdered erythritol or Swerve

Optional: ½ teaspoon ground cinnamon or vanilla bean powder

CUPS

8.5 oz (240 g) Homemade Dark Chocolate (page 16) or 90% dark chocolate

⅔ cup (170 g/6 oz) Toasted Almond -Cashew Butter (recipe above)

¼ cup (15 g/0.5 oz) toasted coconut flakes

If you're a fan of Reese's Peanut Butter Cups, this recipe is for you! Since many people who follow a keto diet also avoid peanuts, these treats are made with a good-for-you homemade alternative: a toasted almond-cashew butter. You'll be surprised at how much it tastes like peanut butter, and—like peanut butter—it's a great match for dark chocolate.

TO MAKE THE TOASTED ALMOND-CASHEW BUTTER: Preheat the oven to 350°F (175°C, or gas mark 4). Spread the almonds and cashews on a baking sheet and bake for 12 to 15 minutes. Watch them carefully because they burn easily.

Remove from the oven, and let them cool for a few minutes. Then add them to a food processor along with the oil. Pulse until smooth: this may take several minutes. Scrape down the sides several times with a rubber spatula if the mixture sticks. Add the salt and, optionally, the erythritol and cinnamon. Pulse again. Reserve ⅔ cup (170 g/6 oz) for this recipe. Spoon any leftover nut butter into a glass container, and store at room temperature for a week or keep refrigerated for up to a month.

TO MAKE THE CUPS: Melt the dark chocolate in a double boiler or in a heatproof bowl placed over a small saucepan filled with 1 cup (235 ml) of water, over medium heat. Remove from the heat and let cool slightly.

Place 8 small paper muffin cups on a tray. Fill each with about 1 tablespoon (15 ml) of chocolate. Let them sit for 10 minutes, and then swirl the chocolate around to cover the sides and to create a bowl shape. Refrigerate for about 10 minutes to harden. When the chocolate is solid, top each cup with about 2 teaspoons of the almond-cashew butter. Flatten with a spoon. Pour another 1 table-spoon (15 ml) of chocolate into each cup and top with the toasted coconut flakes.

NUTRITION FACTS PER SERVING (1 KETO CUP): Total carbs: 7.3 g | Fiber: 3.3 g | Net carbs: 4 g | Protein: 5.2 g | Fat: 31.2 g | Calories: 323 kcal
MACRONUTRIENT RATIO: Calories from carbs (5%), protein (7%), fat (88%)

Refrigerate for 30 minutes to 1 hour, or until solid. Keep the cups refrigerated for up to 1 week or freeze for up to 3 months.

NOTES:

- These make 8 generous servings, but the recipe can be stretched to 16 if you use smaller muffin cups or cut them in half.
- Short on time? Use one or both of these options:

  1. For the filling, use any nut or seed butter. The best options are toasted almond butter or toasted coconut butter. Toasting significantly enhances the nut butter's flavor, making the finished cups even more delicious.

  2. For the coating, use 90% dark chocolate.

SPICY CHOCOLATE BBQ SAUCE, PAGE 164

ABOVE: TOASTED NUT BUTTER, PAGE 169

DIJON MUSTARD, PAGE 162

CHAPTER 8

EXTRAS: *Sauces, Marinades,* AND MUCH MORE

MARINARA SAUCE, PAGE 166

RED PESTO, PAGE/168

KETCHUP, PAGE 161

SPICED BERRY CHIA JAM, PAGE 170

MAYONNAISE, PAGE 163

BECAUSE I WANT TO HAVE AS MUCH CONTROL OVER what I eat as possible, I avoid store-bought products. Most of them contain undesirable additives or hidden sources of sugar that can ruin a low-carb diet. And besides, it's so easy—and far more budget-friendly!—to make your own.

Here you'll find recipes for even more essential keto ingredients you'll use in your low-carb kitchen every day. Bone Broth (page 160) turns up in lots of the soups in this book, and it's a great source of electrolytes, so it's especially important to have a batch on hand if you're in the induction phase of the ketogenic diet. My Mayonnaise (page 163), Ketchup (page 161), and Dijon Mustard (page 162) are all sugar-free, so you can go ahead and slather them on sandwiches and use them in sauces and salad dressings. Keto-friendly, macadamia-based Basil Pesto (page 167) and Red Pesto (page 168) feature in some of my Italian-inflected recipes, and having batches of Spiced Berry Chia Jam (page 170) and Toasted Nut Butter (page 169) on hand means that you've got the ingredients to make all sorts of no-sugar sweet treats, too.

For even more recipes, visit my website at ketodietapp.com/blog and use the filtering tool to see all "homemade basics."

Bone Broth

6 TO 8 CUPS (1.4 TO 1.9 L)
HANDS-ON TIME: 10 MINUTES
OVERALL TIME: 2 HOURS OR MORE

2 medium (120 g/4.2 oz) carrots, peeled and cut into thirds

1 large (150 g/5.3 oz) white onion, halved

4 to 6 cloves garlic, halved

2 large (128 g/4.5 oz) celery stalks, cut into thirds

3.3 pounds (1.5 kg) oxtail or assorted bones (chicken feet, marrowbones, etc.)

2 tablespoons (30 ml) apple cider vinegar or lemon juice

3 bay leaves

3 whole allspice berries

1 tablespoon (17 g/0.6 oz) fine sea salt

2-inch (5-cm) piece turmeric, sliced, or 1 teaspoon ground turmeric

8 to 10 cups (1.9 to 2.4 L) water (enough to cover the bones, no more than ⅔ the capacity of the pressure cooker, ¾ of the Dutch oven, or ¾ of the slow cooker)

Bone broth is your best friend when you're following a keto diet. It's rich both in gelatin and minerals that will ease the nasty symptoms of keto flu, and it's an essential ingredient in soups and stews. Add a little turmeric, either fresh or ground, for extra antioxidants.

Place all the ingredients in the slow cooker. Cover with a lid. Cook on high for 4 to 5 hours or on low for 8 to 10 hours. Remove the oxtail using tongs and shred the meat using a fork (use the cooked meat for quick meals). Place the bones back in the slow cooker and cook on low for up to 48 hours (optional but highly recommended). Once the broth has cooled, strain it through a sieve, and store it without any bones, spices, or vegetables. Keep it in the fridge if you're planning to use it over the next 4 to 5 days. For future uses, store it in small containers and freeze.

NOTES:
- Oxtail is high in fat, and the greasy layer on top—the tallow—will solidify. Simply scrape most of the tallow off and discard or reuse it for cooking.
- If using an Instant Pot/pressure cooker: Set to high pressure, close the lid, and turn the valve to the sealing position. Set the time to 45 minutes. When the program has finished, let the steam release naturally for 15 to 20 minutes, and then turn the valve to venting to release the remaining steam.

NUTRITION FACTS PER 1 CUP (240 ML): Total carbs: 0.9 g | Fiber: 0.2 g | Net carbs: 0.7 g | Protein: 3.6 g | Fat: 6 g | Calories: 72 kcal

MACRONUTRIENT RATIO: Calories from carbs (4%), protein (20%), fat (76%)

NOTE: Nutrition facts, especially protein, in homemade bone broth vary and depend on several factors, such as type of bones used and cooking time.

Ketchup

1 CUP (240 G/8.5 OZ)
HANDS-ON TIME: 5 MINUTES
OVERALL TIME: 15 MINUTES

1 small (60 g/2.1 oz) white onion, cut
    into small pieces
2 cloves garlic, chopped
1 cup (240 g/8.5 oz) unsweetened
    tomato paste
¼ cup (60 ml) apple cider vinegar
⅛ teaspoon allspice
⅛ teaspoon ground cloves
3 to 6 drops liquid stevia
2 tablespoons (20 g/0.7 oz)
    erythritol or Swerve
1 teaspoon salt
Freshly ground black pepper, to
    taste
¼ cup (60 ml) water

Even though we think of it as a "savory" condiment, ketchup's third ingredient is sugar (it appears in ingredient lists as high-fructose corn syrup). And that spells disaster if you're eating keto. But the good news is that you can make your own sugar-free ketchup on the stovetop in just a few minutes. It's surprisingly easy!

Combine all the ingredients in a small saucepan and simmer, covered, over low heat for 5 to 10 minutes. Add a splash of water if the mixture seems too thick. When done, transfer the mixture to a blender and pulse until smooth. Pour the ketchup into a glass jar and store in the fridge for up to a month.

NOTE:
Homemade ketchup is a key ingredient in many other sauces, dressings, and dips, like my Spicy Chocolate BBQ Sauce (page 164)!

NUTRITION FACTS PER SERVING (1 TABLESPOON/15 G/0.5 OZ): Total carbs: 1 g | Fiber: 0.2 g | Net carbs: 0.8 g |
Protein: 0.2 g | Fat: 0 g | Calories: 5 kcal
MACRONUTRIENT RATIO: Calories from carbs (77%), protein (7%), fat (6%)

Dijon Mustard

2 CUPS (480 G/16.9 OZ)
HANDS-ON TIME: 10 MINUTES
OVERALL TIME: 15 TO 20 MINUTES

1 medium (110 g/3.9 oz) onion

2 cloves garlic

1 cup (240 ml) dry white wine, or
substitute with ¼ cup (60 ml)
vinegar and ¾ cup (180 ml) water

¼ cup (60 ml) white wine vinegar

½ cup (120 ml) water

1 cup (120 g/4.2 oz) mustard
powder/ground mustard seeds

1 teaspoon ground turmeric

Optional: 3 to 5 dashes Tabasco or
other sugar-free hot sauce

5 to 10 drops liquid stevia

2 tablespoons (30 ml) extra-virgin
olive oil (or macadamia or
avocado oil)

1 teaspoon salt

I never even considered making mustard at home until I started eating low-carb. But now I'd never go back to the mass-produced kind! Like the sugar-free Ketchup (page 161), this can easily be made on the stovetop in a few minutes, and it improves with age when you store it in the fridge.

Peel and roughly chop the onion and garlic and place them in a nonreactive saucepan (see Notes). Pour in the wine, vinegar, and water, and bring to a boil over medium heat. Simmer for about 5 minutes.

Cool and strain the mixture, discarding the solids. Place the mustard powder into a saucepan and add the strained liquid. Mix until well combined. Cook over medium-low heat until it thickens, about 2 to 5 minutes. Add the turmeric, Tabasco (if using), stevia, oil, and salt.

Mix until well combined. Store in a jar in the refrigerator for up to 6 months. The mustard will taste best after a few weeks of aging.

NOTES:
- You can make different types of mustard by adding a variety of optional ingredients. Try horseradish, fresh herbs, or whole-grain mustard seeds.
- What is a nonreactive saucepan? It's a saucepan made of a material that will not react with acidic ingredients. For example, stainless steel is nonreactive, while copper is a reactive material that will easily erode if used with acidic ingredients like lemon juice or vinegar.

NUTRITION FACTS PER SERVING (1 TABLESPOON/15 G/0.5 OZ): Total carbs: 1.1 g | Fiber: 0.4 g | Net carbs: 0.7 g | Protein: 0.8 g | Fat: 1.7 g | Calories: 27 kcal
MACRONUTRIENT RATIO: Calories from carbs (13%), protein (15%), fat (72%)

Mayonnaise

2 CUPS (480 G/16.9 OZ)
HANDS-ON TIME: 15 MINUTES
OVERALL TIME: 15 MINUTES

- 2 pastured egg yolks, at room temperature
- 2 teaspoons (10 g/0.2 oz) Dijon mustard
- 2 tablespoons (30 ml) apple cider vinegar, divided
- 1½ cups (360 ml) mild olive oil (or macadamia, avocado, or walnut oil)
- 2 tablespoons (30 ml) fresh lemon juice
- ½ teaspoon sea salt
- Optional: 2 tablespoons (30 ml) whey or powder from 1 to 2 probiotic capsules

Like Bone Broth (page 160), mayonnaise is a keto staple. Somehow it's gotten a reputation for being difficult to make, but nothing could be further from the truth. This recipe is proof! And if you ferment your mayo by adding whey or the contents of a couple of probiotic capsules to it, it'll stay fresh for much longer.

Place the yolks, Dijon mustard, and 1 tablespoon (15 ml) of the vinegar into a bowl, and mix until well combined.

Drizzle in the oil until the mixture starts to look more like the consistency of mayonnaise. Steadily pour in the oil until all of it is incorporated. Keep mixing until the mayo reaches the desired thickness. If it doesn't seem thick enough, add a bit more oil.

Mix in the lemon juice and the remaining 1 tablespoon (15 ml) vinegar—this will turn the mixture a light yellow color. Season with salt. If you think the consistency is too thick, add a few drops of water or lemon juice. Transfer the mayonnaise to a glass container and seal tightly. You can store it in the fridge for up to 1 week.

Optionally, mix in the whey and combine with the mayo. Transfer the mayonnaise to a jar, cover loosely with a lid or a cloth, and let it sit on a kitchen counter for 8 hours. This is essential in order to activate the enzymes that will keep your mayo fresh. After 8 hours, refrigerate and use within the next 3 months.

NOTES:
Convert your mayo into aioli or tartar sauce in a few easy steps:
- AIOLI: Add 2 to 4 cloves of minced garlic to the prepared mayonnaise.
- TARTAR SAUCE: Mix ½ cup (110 g/3.9 oz) of the prepared mayonnaise with 2 small (50 g/1.8 oz) grated pickles, 2 tablespoons (30 ml) lemon juice, ¼ teaspoon salt, and ⅛ teaspoon black pepper. Optionally, add 1 tablespoon (4 g/0.1 oz) chopped fresh dill or parsley.

NUTRITION FACTS PER SERVING (1 TABLESPOON/15 G/0.5 OZ): Total carbs: 0.1 g | Fiber: 0 g | Net carbs: 0.1 g | Protein: 0.2 g | Fat: 12.5 g | Calories: 111 kcal
MACRONUTRIENT RATIO: Calories from carbs (0%), protein (1%), fat (99%)

Spicy Chocolate BBQ Sauce

1½ CUPS (360 G/12.7 OZ)
HANDS-ON TIME: 10 MINUTES
OVERALL TIME: 10 MINUTES

2 cloves garlic, crushed

1 cup (240 g/8.5 oz) Ketchup
(page 161)

2 tablespoons (30 ml) apple cider
vinegar

2 tablespoons (30 ml) coconut
aminos or fish sauce

2 tablespoons (10 g/0.4 oz)
unsweetened cacao powder

2 tablespoons (20 g/0.7 oz)
erythritol or Swerve

5 to 10 drops stevia

2 teaspoons paprika (regular or
smoked)

1 teaspoon chile powder (mild or hot,
to taste)

2 tablespoons (30 g/1.1 oz) butter,
ghee, or extra-virgin olive oil

½ teaspoon smoked salt or regular
sea salt

Like so many other condiments, store-bought barbecue sauce contains sugar. Skip it and whip up this zingy keto version instead. There's nothing you can't do with it: Smear it on ribs, use it as a meat marinade, or dunk raw veggies into it.

Place all the ingredients in a saucepan and cook over medium heat for 5 to 10 minutes. Transfer to a glass jar and keep in the fridge for up to a month.

NOTE:
Coconut aminos are a healthier alternative to soy sauce and are often recommended as a healthy soy sauce substitute on paleo diets. Soy products should be eaten in moderation, and some of them should be avoided completely. Unfortunately, most soy products come from genetically modified (GMO) soybeans, and how GMO products affect health is still unclear. If you decide to use soy products, find ones that are made from non-GMO, fermented, unprocessed soy and that are gluten-free.

NUTRITION FACTS PER SERVING (1 TABLESPOON/15 G/0.5 OZ): Total carbs: 1.3 g | Fiber: 0.4 g | Net carbs: 0.9 g | Protein: 0.3 g | Fat: 1.1 g | Calories: 15 kcal
MACRONUTRIENT RATIO: Calories from carbs (24%), protein (8%), fat (68%)

Sweet & Sour BBQ Sauce

MAKES: ABOUT 4 CUPS (900 G/2 LB)
HANDS-ON TIME: 15 MINUTES
OVERALL TIME: 6 HOURS

2 tablespoons (30 g/1.1 oz) ghee or
   lard
1 large (150 g/5.3 oz) yellow onion,
   diced
4 cloves garlic, minced
2 medium (28 g/1 oz) jalapeño
   peppers, seeds and membranes
   removed
1½ cups (360 g/12.7 oz) canned
   tomatoes
½ cup (125 g/4.4 oz) unsweetened
   tomato paste
½ cup (120 ml) apple cider vinegar
   or coconut vinegar
¼ cup (60 ml) coconut aminos
¼ cup (50 g/1.8 oz) granulated
   erythritol or Swerve
2 teaspoons paprika (sweet or
   smoked)
2 teaspoons mustard powder
1 teaspoon celery seeds
½ teaspoon chili powder
½ teaspoon black pepper
⅛ teaspoon ground cloves
⅛ teaspoon ground allspice
1 teaspoon fine sea salt, or to taste
2 teaspoons extra-virgin olive oil
Optional: Few drops of liquid stevia

This sweet, tangy, easy-to-prepare BBQ sauce is the perfect way
to dress up juicy ribs, fork-tender pulled pork, and comforting
meat stews.

Preheat a slow cooker to low. In a pan greased with ghee, cook the
onion over medium-low heat for about 10 minutes, until browned and
fragrant. Add the garlic and cook for another minute.

Place the browned onion and garlic in the preheated slow cooker.
Add all the remaining ingredients, apart from the olive oil and stevia
(if using), and cook for 6 hours. When done, turn off the heat and let it
cool for an hour. Add the olive oil and optional stevia. Using a blender,
process the sauce until smooth. Transfer to a glass jar and keep in
the fridge for up to a month. For longer storage, spoon the sauce into
an ice cube tray and freeze for 2 hours. Pop out the cubes, place in a
freezer bag, and store in the freezer for up to 6 months.

NUTRITION FACTS PER SERVING (1 TABLESPOON/15 G/0.5 OZ): Total carbs: 1 g | Fiber: 0.2 g | Net carbs: 0.8 g |
Protein: 0.2 g | Fat: 1 g | Calories: 13 kcal
MACRONUTRIENT RATIO: Calories from carbs (23%), protein (5%), fat (72%)

Marinara Sauce

2 CUPS (490 G/17.3 OZ)
HANDS-ON TIME: 5 MINUTES
OVERALL TIME: 5 MINUTES

1 cup (150 g/5.3 oz) cherry tomatoes
½ cup (20 g/0.7 oz) fresh basil
2 cloves garlic
1 small (30 g/1.1 oz) shallot
4 tablespoons (60 g/2.2 oz)
    unsweetened tomato paste
¼ cup (60 ml) extra-virgin olive oil
¼ teaspoon salt
Freshly ground pepper, to taste

Toss this simple, herbed sauce with zucchini noodles, dip warm, low-carb bread into it, or better yet, use it to make Breakfast Pizza Waffles (page 28) Pizza Two Ways (page 124), or the Easy Italian Breakfast Bake (page 37).

Wash and dry the tomatoes and basil. Peel the garlic and shallot. Add all the ingredients to a food processor and process until smooth. If you prefer a chunky texture, leave some tomatoes and basil aside to dice and add to the smooth sauce after it's blended. When done, store in an airtight container in the fridge for up to a week.

NUTRITION FACTS PER SERVING (¼ CUP/60 G/2.1 OZ): Total carbs: 3.5 g | Fiber: 0.8 g | Net carbs: 2.6 g | Protein: 0.7 g | Fat: 9.8 g | Calories: 101 kcal
MACRONUTRIENT RATIO: Calories from carbs (10%), protein (3%), fat (87%)

Basil Pesto

1 CUP (240 G/8.5 OZ)
HANDS-ON TIME: 5 MINUTES
OVERALL TIME: 5 MINUTES

2 cups (30 g/1.1 oz) fresh basil

⅓ cup (45 g/1.6 oz) macadamia nuts
   or sunflower seeds

2 tablespoons (15 g/0.5 oz) pine nuts
   or more sunflower seeds

4 cloves garlic, minced

1 teaspoon fresh lemon zest

1 tablespoon (15 ml) fresh lemon
   juice

½ cup (120 ml) extra-virgin olive oil

Optional: ⅓ cup (30 g/1.1 oz) grated
   Parmesan cheese

Salt and pepper, to taste

Pesto is naturally low-carb, but why buy it premade when you can blitz it up in seconds with a few simple ingredients? This recipe features a base of macadamia nuts, which provide plenty of heart-healthy fats, and better still, you can easily tweak it to make it nut- or dairy-free. Dress up zucchini noodles with a dollop of it, or use it in my Stuffed Avocados Two Ways (page 73).

Place all the ingredients except the seasoning in a blender. Process until smooth, then season with sea salt and black pepper to taste.

You can keep your pesto in the fridge for 1 to 2 weeks. Whenever you use the pesto, always remember to add a thin layer of olive oil on top before you place it back in the fridge. To preserve pesto for longer, spoon it into an ice cube tray and place in the freezer. Once frozen, empty the ice cube tray into a resealable plastic bag. Keep your frozen pesto cubes for up to 6 months.

NUTRITION FACTS PER SERVING (1 TABLESPOON/15 G/0.5 OZ): Total carbs: 0.9 g | Fiber: 0.3 g | Net carbs: 0.6 g | Protein: 0.5 g | Fat: 9.9 g | Calories: 92 kcal
MACRONUTRIENT RATIO: Calories from carbs (2%), protein (2%), fat (96%)

Red Pesto

2 CUPS (470 G/16.6 OZ)
HANDS-ON TIME: 5 MINUTES
OVERALL TIME: 5 MINUTES

¼ cup (25 g/0.9 oz) pitted green or
   black olives
½ cup (67 g/2.4 oz) macadamia nuts
2 tablespoons (20 g/0.7 oz) pine nuts
1 cup (110 g/3.9 oz) sun-dried
   tomatoes, drained
6 cloves garlic, sliced
1 tablespoon (15 ml) fresh lemon
   juice or apple cider vinegar
¼ cup (63 g/2.2 oz) unsweetened
   tomato paste
2 cups (30 g/1.1 oz) fresh basil leaves
½ cup (120 ml) extra-virgin olive oil
¼ teaspoon fine sea salt
¼ teaspoon black pepper
Optional: ½ cup (45 g/1.6 oz) grated
   Parmesan cheese

There's almost always a jar of Red Pesto front and center in my fridge. I use it nearly every day, because it's the easiest ever way to add zing to casseroles, soups, salads, and much more. It's essential for Keto Tortillas (page 11), and veggie-rich Ratatouille Soup (page 64), and it's a great topping for keto pizza (see Pizza Two Ways, page 124).

Place all the ingredients in a food processor and pulse until smooth. Alternatively, use a mortar and pestle to crush all the ingredients into a smooth paste. Transfer to a jar and refrigerate.

You can keep your pesto in the fridge for 1 to 2 weeks. Whenever you use the pesto, always remember to add a thin layer of olive oil on top before you place it back in the fridge. To preserve pesto for longer, spoon it into an ice cube tray and place in the freezer. Once frozen, empty the ice cube tray into a resealable plastic bag. Keep your frozen pesto cubes for up to 6 months.

NUTRITION FACTS PER SERVING (1 TABLESPOON/15 G/0.5 OZ): Total carbs: 1.6 g | Fiber: 0.5 g | Net carbs: 1.1 g | Protein: 0.5 g | Fat: 6.1 g | Calories: 61 kcal
MACRONUTRIENT RATIO: Calories from carbs (7%), protein (4%), fat (89%)

Toasted Nut Butter

1½ CUPS (400 G/14.1 OZ)
HANDS-ON TIME: 10 MINUTES
OVERALL TIME: 25 TO 35 MINUTES

1 cup (130 g/4.6 oz) macadamia nuts

1 cup (150 g/5.3 oz) blanched
almonds

2 cups (120 g/4.2 oz) desiccated
flaked coconut

Macadamia nuts and almonds are high in healthy monounsaturated fats, not to mention a whole host of vitamins and minerals (B vitamins, potassium, and lots more). Add some desiccated coconut, blitz in your food processor, and you've got a nut butter you can spread on Keto Tortillas (page 11) or use to make Cookie Dough Mousse (page 147). Try adding 1 tablespoon (15 g/0.5 oz) of it to a smoothie, too.

Preheat the oven to 350°F (175°C, or gas mark 4). Spread the nuts and flaked coconut evenly on a baking sheet and transfer to the oven. Bake for 12 to 15 minutes, until slightly brown. Keep an eye on the nuts; if they burn, they will have an unpleasant bitter taste.

Remove from the oven and let cool for 10 minutes. Place the cooled nuts and coconut in a food processor and pulse until smooth and creamy. At first, the mixture will be dry. Scrape down the sides of your processor several times with a rubber spatula if the mixture sticks. This may take up to 10 minutes depending on your processor.

Spoon the nut butter into a glass container and store at room temperature for 1 week or refrigerate for up to 3 months.

NUTRITION FACTS PER SERVING (2 TABLESPOONS/32 G/1.1 OZ): Total carbs: 5.9 g | Fiber: 3.6 g | Net carbs: 2.3 g | Protein: 4 g | Fat: 20.2 g | Calories: 206 kcal
MACRONUTRIENT RATIO: Calories from carbs (4%), protein (8%), fat (88%)

Spiced Berry Chia Jam

2 CUPS (480 G/16.9 OZ)
HANDS-ON TIME: 10 MINUTES
OVERALL TIME: 20 MINUTES

1 cup (140 g/4.9 oz) strawberries
1 cup (125 g/4.4 oz) raspberries
1 cup (140 g/4.9 oz) blackberries
½ cup (75 g/2.6 oz) blueberries
½ teaspoon ground ginger or
   1 teaspoon freshly grated ginger
½ teaspoon ground cinnamon
1 tablespoon (6 g/0.2 oz) orange zest
¼ teaspoon ground cloves
1 star anise
2 tablespoons (20 g/0.7 oz)
   erythritol or Swerve
10 to 15 drops liquid stevia
2 tablespoons (16 g/0.5 oz) chia
   seeds

You'll never buy jam from the supermarket again once you've made this naturally vegan chia jam! The chia seeds take the place of gelatin when it comes to creating a thick, spreadable texture (and they add a little extra fiber to the mix, too). Spread a dollop on a buttered Keto Sourdough Bun (page 10) or use it to top Chocolate Chip Pancakes (page 42).

Wash the berries and place in a saucepan. Add all the remaining ingredients except for the chia seeds. Bring to a boil and then lower the heat. Cook for 5 to 8 minutes. Remove from the heat. Remove and discard the star anise.

Add the chia seeds and mix well. Let the jam sit for about 15 minutes before transferring to a lidded jar. Store in the fridge for up to 2 weeks.

NUTRITION FACTS PER SERVING (2 TABLESPOONS/40 G/1.4 OZ): Total carbs: 4.8 g | Fiber: 2.2 g | Net carbs: 2.6 g | Protein: 0.7 g | Fat: 0.6 g | Calories: 24 kcal
MACRONUTRIENT RATIO: Calories from carbs (57%), protein (14%), fat (29%)

Chimichurri

ABOUT 1 CUP (240 G/8.5 OZ)
HANDS-ON TIME: 5 MINUTES
OVERALL TIME: 5 MINUTES

1 large (60 g/2.1 oz) bunch fresh parsley

¼ cup (15 g/0.5 oz) chopped fresh oregano

4 cloves garlic, chopped

1 small (5 g/0.2 oz) red chile pepper, seeds removed

2 tablespoons (30 ml) apple cider vinegar or fresh lime juice

½ cup (120 ml) extra-virgin olive oil

½ teaspoon salt

¼ teaspoon black pepper

Never had chimichurri before? It's a flavorful, traditional Argentinian sauce made with fresh green parsley, fragrant oregano, garlic, chile, and vinegar or citrus juice. It's often served atop steak, and it makes a great marinade, too, but don't reserve it for meat only: it's the perfect high-fat salad dressing!

Simply place all the ingredients in a blender and process until smooth. Store sealed in the fridge for up to a week.

NUTRITION FACTS PER SERVING (2 TABLESPOONS/30 G/1.1 OZ): Total carbs: 2.4 g | Fiber: 1 g | Net carbs: 1.4 g | Protein: 0.4 g | Fat: 13.8 g | Calories: 133 kcal
MACRONUTRIENT RATIO: Calories from carbs (4%), protein (1%), fat (95%)

About the Author

Martina Slajerova is a health and food blogger living in the United Kingdom. She holds a degree in economics and worked in auditing, but has always been passionate about nutrition and healthy living. Martina loves food, science, photography, and creating new recipes. She is a firm believer in low-carb living and regular exercise. As a science geek, she bases her views on valid research and has firsthand experience of what it means to be on a low-carb diet. Both are reflected on her blog, in her KetoDiet apps, and in this book.

The KetoDiet is an ongoing project she started with her partner in 2012 and includes *The KetoDiet Cookbook*, *Sweet and Savory Fat Bombs*, *Quick Keto Meals in 30 Minutes or Less*, *Keto Slow Cooker & One-Pot Meals*, and the KetoDiet apps for the iPad and iPhone (www.ketodietapp.com). When creating recipes, she doesn't focus on just the carb content: you won't find any processed foods, unhealthy vegetable oils, or artificial sweeteners in her recipes.

This book and the KetoDiet apps are for people who follow a healthy low-carb lifestyle. Martina's mission is to help you reach your goals, whether it's your dream weight or simply eating healthy food. You can find even more low-carb recipes, diet plans, and information about the keto diet on her blog: www.ketodietapp.com/blog.

Acknowledgments

To my amazing readers, thank you so much for your continuous love and support. I hope my book will inspire you to create even more healthy and delicious low-carb dishes!

To Nikos, my soul mate and the best partner I could have ever wished for. You helped me turn my passion into a job I love. Thank you for always being there for me!

To my family and friends, who have always believed in me. They have made the biggest impression on who I am today.

To the KetoDiet team—all the amazing people I am so fortunate to be working with. You make a real difference in people's lives every day!

I'd also like to thank the fabulous team at Fair Winds Press, who always put so much hard work into making this a reality. It's been an absolute pleasure working with you! Special thanks to Jill Alexander, Renae Haines, Heather Godin, Lydia Jopp, Jenna Patton, and Megan Buckley.

Index

A

Abundance Breakfast Bowls, 27
Almond Bliss Bars, 143
Avocado-Egg Stuffed Bacon Cups, 47

B

Bacon-Wrapped Beef Patties with "Chimiole," 82
Bacon-Wrapped Chorizo Meatloaf with Caramelized Cauliflower, 128
Baked Jalapeño Popper Dip, 51
Basil Pesto, 167
Beef Bourguignon, 131
Beef Short Ribs with Coleslaw, 130
Bone Broth, 160
Boston Cream Pie, 150–151
Breakfast Egg Muffins Two Ways, 24
Breakfast Pizza Waffles, 28
Breakfast Sausage Guac Stacks, 34
Broccoli & Mushroom Alfredo Casserole, 94
Brownie Almond Cheesecake Bars, 152
Butter Chicken, 106

C

Cajun Andouille Gumbo, 101
Carne Asada Salad, 71
Carrot Cake Oatmeal, 39
Cauliflower Rice Three Ways, 13
Cheese-Stuffed Greek Bifteki, 137
Cheeseburger Soup, 59
Chewy Pumpkin and Chocolate Chip Cookies, 148
Chicken Caesar Salad with Poached Egg, 72
Chicken Piccata, 110
Chimichurri, 171
Chocolate and Raspberry Truffles, 142
Chocolate Chip Pancakes, 42
Chorizo & Kale Hash, 36
Clam Chowder, 63
Cookie Dough Mousse, 147
Coq au Vin, 105
Creamy Dark Hot Chocolate, 154
Creamy "Potato" Soup, 65
Crispy Chicken with Olives and Lemon, 109
Crispy Ranch Chicken Wings, 53
Czech Butter Cake, 144

D

Dairy-free recipes
    Abundance Breakfast Bowls, 27
    Almond Bliss Bars, 143
    Avocado-Egg Stuffed Bacon Cups, 47
    Bacon-Wrapped Beef Patties with "Chimiole," 82
    Bacon-Wrapped Chorizo Meatloaf with Caramelized Cauliflower, 128
    Basil Pesto, 167

Beef Bourguignon, 131
Beef Short Ribs with Coleslaw, 130
Bone Broth, 160
Boston Cream Pie, 150–151
Breakfast Egg Muffins Two Ways, 24
Breakfast Sausage Guac Stacks, 34
Cajun Andouille Gumbo, 101
Carne Asada Salad, 71
Carrot Cake Oatmeal, 39
Chewy Pumpkin and Chocolate Chip Cookies, 148
Chimichurri, 171
Chocolate and Raspberry Truffles, 142
Chocolate Chip Pancakes, 42
Chorizo & Kale Hash, 36
Coq au Vin, 105
Creamy Dark Hot Chocolate, 154
Creamy "Potato" Soup, 65
Crispy Chicken with Olives and Lemon, 109
Dijon Mustard, 162
Eggs Florentine in Portobello Mushrooms, 22–23
Fat-Fueled Smoothie Two Ways, 43
Flavored Butter Twelve Ways, 14–15
Fluffy Cocoa & Berry Omelet, 41
Greek Meatball Soup, 60
Green Shakshuka, 31
Harissa Fish Tray Bake, 100
Healthy Deconstructed Hamburgers, 127
Healthy Fish Sticks with Tartar Sauce, 97
Homemade Dark Chocolate Three Ways, 16–17
Hungarian Goulash, 66
Ketchup, 161
Keto Kung Pao Chicken, 114
Keto "Peanut" Butter Cups, 156–157
Keto Tortillas Three Ways, 11
Key Lime Pie in a Jar, 145
Lamb Vindaloo, 135
Marinara Sauce, 166
Mayonnaise, 163
"No-Tella" Granola, 40
Peri Peri Roasted Nuts, 49
Pork Pot Roast with Vegetables, 123
Pork Schnitzel with Zesty Slaw, 116
Raspberry Electrolyte Limeade, 155
Red Pesto, 168
Roast Duck with Braised Cabbage, 113
Salisbury Steak with Quick Mash, 132
Salmon Niçoise Salad, 69
Skillet Berry Crumble, 146
Slovak Sauerkraut Soup, 56
Snickerdoodle Crème Brûlée, 153
Southern Duck Deviled Eggs, 48
Spanish Eggs, 21
Spiced Berry Chia Jam, 170

Spiced Coconut Granola Bars, 89
Spicy Chocolate BBQ Sauce, 164
Steak Fajitas with Avocado Salsa Verde, 133
Stuffed Avocados Two Ways, 73
Sushi: Spicy Tuna Rolls, 99
Sweet Cinnamon Rolls, 38
Sweet & Sour BBQ Sauce, 165
Thai Curry Chicken Tray Bake, 102
Tiramisu Ice Bombs, 140
Toasted Nut Butter, 169
Turkey Souvlaki with Supergreens Salad, 115
Vanilla-Keto Ice Cream, 141
Vanilla Panna Cotta with Strawberry Coulis, 149
Dijon Mustard, 162

E

Easy Italian Breakfast Bake, 37
Egg-free recipes
    Almond Bliss Bars, 143
    Bacon-Wrapped Beef Patties with "Chimiole," 82
    Basil Pesto, 167
    Beef Bourguignon, 131
    Bone Broth, 160
    Broccoli & Mushroom Alfredo Casserole, 94
    Butter Chicken, 106
    Cajun Andouille Gumbo, 101
    Carne Asada Salad, 71
    Carrot Cake Oatmeal, 39
    Chicken Piccata, 110
    Chimichurri, 171
    Chocolate and Raspberry Truffles, 142
    Chorizo & Kale Hash, 36
    Clam Chowder, 63
    Cookie Dough Mousse, 147
    Coq au Vin, 105
    Creamy Dark Hot Chocolate, 154
    Creamy "Potato" Soup, 65
    Crispy Chicken with Olives and Lemon, 109
    Dijon Mustard, 162
    Easy Italian Breakfast Bake, 37
    Eggplant Parma Ham Rolls, 78
    Fat-Fueled Smoothie Two Ways, 43
    Flavored Butter Twelve Ways, 14–15
    Greek Breakfast Hash, 35
    Greek Briam, 93
    Ham and Cheese Fat Bombs, 46
    Harissa Fish Tray Bake, 100
    Homemade Dark Chocolate Three Ways, 16–17
    Ketchup, 161
    Keto Cheese Sauce Three Ways, 12
    Keto Kung Pao Chicken, 114
    Keto "Peanut" Butter Cups, 156–157
    Keto Tortillas Three Ways, 11

Key Lime Pie in a Jar, 145
Lamb Vindaloo, 135
Marinara Sauce, 166
Masala Cauli-Rice with Grilled
    Halloumi, 96
Mexican Chicken Bowls, 85
Peri Peri Roasted Nuts, 49
Pizza Two Ways, 124–125
Pork Pot Roast with Vegetables, 123
Raspberry Electrolyte Limeade, 155
Ratatouille Soup, 64
Red Pesto, 168
Roast Duck with Braised Cabbage,
    113
Shepherd's Pie, 134
Skillet Berry Crumble, 146
Slovak Sauerkraut Soup, 56
Speedy Cauliflower-n-Cheese, 117
Speedy Keto Crackers, 50
Spiced Berry Chia Jam, 170
Spicy Chocolate BBQ Sauce, 164
Steak Fajitas with Avocado Salsa
    Verde, 133
Stuffed Avocados Two Ways, 73
Sweet & Sour BBQ Sauce, 165
Thai Curry Chicken Tray Bake, 102
Tiramisu Ice Bombs, 140
Toasted Nut Butter, 169
Turkey Souvlaki with Supergreens
    Salad, 115
Vanilla Panna Cotta with Strawberry
    Coulis, 149
Zucchini Lasagna, 81
Eggplant Parma Ham Rolls, 78
Eggs Florentine in Portobello
    Mushrooms, 22–23
Electrolyte-high recipes
    Abundance Breakfast Bowls, 27
    Avocado-Egg Stuffed Bacon Cups, 47
    Bacon-Wrapped Beef Patties with
        "Chimiole," 82
    Bacon-Wrapped Chorizo Meatloaf
        with Caramelized Cauliflower,
        128
    Basil Pesto, 167
    Beef Bourguignon, 131
    Beef Short Ribs with Coleslaw, 130
    Bone Broth, 160
    Boston Cream Pie, 150–151
    Breakfast Sausage Guac Stacks, 34
    Broccoli & Mushroom Alfredo
        Casserole, 94
    Brownie Almond Cheesecake Bars,
        152
    Butter Chicken, 106
    Cajun Andouille Gumbo, 101
    Carne Asada Salad, 71
    Cheese-Stuffed Greek Bifteki, 137
    Cheeseburger Soup, 59
    Chewy Pumpkin and Chocolate Chip
        Cookies, 148
    Chicken Caesar Salad with Poached
        Egg, 72
    Chicken Piccata, 110
    Chimichurri, 171
    Chocolate Chip Pancakes, 42
    Coq au Vin, 105
    Creamy Dark Hot Chocolate, 154
    Crispy Chicken with Olives and
        Lemon, 109

Crispy Ranch Chicken Wings, 53
Easy Italian Breakfast Bake, 37
Eggplant Parma Ham Rolls, 78
Eggplant Parma Ham Rolls, 78
Eggs Florentine in Portobello
    Mushrooms, 22–23
Fat-Fueled Smoothie Two Ways, 43
Greek Briam, 93
Greek Meatball Soup, 60
Green Shakshuka, 31
Harissa Fish Tray Bake, 100
Healthy Deconstructed Hamburgers,
    127
Healthy Fish Sticks with Tartar Sauce,
    97
Hungarian Goulash, 66
Induction Carbonara, 119
Italian Sausage Frittata, 32
Keto Kung Pao Chicken, 114
Key Lime Pie in a Jar, 145
Lamb Vindaloo, 135
Masala Cauli-Rice with Grilled
    Halloumi, 96
Mexican Chicken Bowls, 85
Moussaka, 136
"No-Tella" Granola, 40
Peri Peri Roasted Nuts, 49
Pork Carnitas (Mexican Pulled Pork),
    120
Pork Pot Roast with Vegetables, 123
Pork Schnitzel with Zesty Slaw, 116
Ranch Salad in a Jar, 70
Raspberry Electrolyte Limeade, 155
Ratatouille Soup, 64
Red Pesto, 168
Roast Duck with Braised Cabbage,
    113
Salisbury Steak with Quick Mash, 132
Salmon Niçoise Salad, 69
Shepherd's Pie, 134
Slovak Sauerkraut Soup, 56
Spanish Eggs, 21
Speedy Cauliflower-n-Cheese, 117
Speedy Keto Crackers, 50
Steak Fajitas with Avocado Salsa
    Verde, 133
Stuffed Avocados Two Ways, 73
Sushi: Spicy Tuna Rolls, 99
Taco Frittata, 79
Thai Curry Chicken Tray Bake, 102
Toasted Nut Butter, 169
Turkey Nuggets with Kale Slaw &
    Italian Dressing, 84
Turkey Souvlaki with Supergreens
    Salad, 115
Zucchini Lasagna, 81

F
Fat-Fueled Smoothie Two Ways, 43
Flavored Butter Twelve Ways, 14–15
Fluffy Cocoa & Berry Omelet, 41

G
Greek Breakfast Hash, 35
Greek Briam, 93
Greek Meatball Soup, 60
Greek Zucchini and Feta Fritters, 80
Green Shakshuka, 31

H
Ham and Cheese Fat Bombs, 46
Ham & Cheese Bread Rolls, 86
Harissa Fish Tray Bake, 100
Healthy Deconstructed Hamburgers,
    127
Healthy Fish Sticks with Tartar Sauce, 97
Homemade Dark Chocolate Three Ways,
    16–17
Hungarian Goulash, 66

I
Induction Carbonara, 119
Induction-friendly recipes
    Abundance Breakfast Bowls, 27
    Avocado-Egg Stuffed Bacon Cups, 47
    Bacon-Wrapped Beef Patties with
        "Chimiole," 82
    Bacon-Wrapped Chorizo Meatloaf
        with Caramelized Cauliflower,
        128
    Baked Jalapeño Popper Dip, 51
    Basil Pesto, 167
    Beef Bourguignon, 131
    Beef Short Ribs with Coleslaw, 130
    Bone Broth, 160
    Breakfast Egg Muffins Two Ways, 24
    Breakfast Sausage Guac Stacks, 34
    Broccoli & Mushroom Alfredo
        Casserole, 94
    Butter Chicken, 106
    Cajun Andouille Gumbo, 101
    Carne Asada Salad, 71
    Cheese-Stuffed Greek Bifteki, 137
    Cheeseburger Soup, 59
    Chicken Caesar Salad with Poached
        Egg, 72
    Chicken Piccata, 110
    Chimichurri, 171
    Chorizo & Kale Hash, 36
    Clam Chowder, 63
    Coq au Vin, 105
    Creamy "Potato" Soup, 65
    Crispy Chicken with Olives and
        Lemon, 109
    Crispy Ranch Chicken Wings, 53
    Dijon Mustard, 162
    Easy Italian Breakfast Bake, 37
    Eggplant Parma Ham Rolls, 78
    Eggs Florentine in Portobello Mush-
        rooms, 22–23
    Fat-Fueled Smoothie Two Ways, 43
    Flavored Butter Twelve Ways, 14–15
    Greek Breakfast Hash, 35
    Greek Briam, 93
    Greek Meatball Soup, 60
    Greek Zucchini and Feta Fritters, 80
    Green Shakshuka, 31
    Ham and Cheese Fat Bombs, 46
    Harissa Fish Tray Bake, 100
    Healthy Deconstructed Hamburgers,
        127
    Healthy Fish Sticks with Tartar Sauce,
        97
    Hungarian Goulash, 66
    Italian Sausage Frittata, 32
    Ketchup, 161
    Keto Cheese Sauce Three Ways, 12
    Keto Kung Pao Chicken, 114
    Lamb Vindaloo, 135

Marinara Sauce, 166
Masala Cauli-Rice with Grilled
    Halloumi, 96
Mayonnaise, 163
Mexican Chicken Bowls, 85
Moussaka, 136
Peri Peri Roasted Nuts, 49
Pizza Two Ways, 124–125
Pork Carnitas (Mexican Pulled Pork),
    120
Pork Pot Roast with Vegetables, 123
Pork Schnitzel with Zesty Slaw, 116
Ranch Salad in a Jar, 70
Raspberry Electrolyte Limeade, 155
Ratatouille Soup, 64
Red Pesto, 168
Roast Duck with Braised Cabbage,
    113
Salisbury Steak with Quick Mash, 132
Salmon Niçoise Salad, 69
Shepherd's Pie, 134
Slovak Sauerkraut Soup, 56
Southern Duck Deviled Eggs, 48
Spanish Eggs, 21
Speedy Cauliflower-n-Cheese, 117
Spiced Berry Chia Jam, 170
Spicy Chocolate BBQ Sauce, 164
Steak Fajitas with Avocado Salsa
    Verde, 133
Stuffed Avocados Two Ways, 73
Sushi: Spicy Tuna Rolls, 99
Taco Frittata, 79
Thai Curry Chicken Tray Bake, 102
Toasted Nut Butter, 169
Turkey Nuggets with Kale Slaw &
    Italian Dressing, 84
Turkey Souvlaki with Supergreens
    Salad, 115
Zucchini Lasagna, 81
Intermittent-fasting recipes
    Abundance Breakfast Bowls, 27
    Almond Bliss Bars, 143
    Bacon-Wrapped Beef Patties with
        "Chimiole," 82
    Bacon-Wrapped Chorizo Meatloaf
        with Caramelized Cauliflower,
        128
    Beef Bourguignon, 131
    Bone Broth, 160
    Butter Chicken, 106
    Carne Asada Salad, 71
    Cheese-Stuffed Greek Bifteki, 137
    Cheeseburger Soup, 59
    Chicken Caesar Salad with Poached
        Egg, 72
    Chocolate and Raspberry Truffles,
        142
    Chorizo & Kale Hash, 36
    Coq au Vin, 105
    Creamy Dark Hot Chocolate, 154
    Crispy Chicken with Olives and
        Lemon, 109
    Eggs Florentine in Portobello
        Mushrooms, 22–23
    Greek Breakfast Hash, 35
    Greek Meatball Soup, 60
    Ham and Cheese Fat Bombs, 46
    Healthy Fish Sticks with Tartar Sauce,
        97
    Lamb Vindaloo, 135

Mexican Chicken Bowls, 85
Moussaka, 136
Pork Carnitas (Mexican Pulled Pork),
    120
Pork Schnitzel with Zesty Slaw, 116
Raspberry Electrolyte Limeade, 155
Roast Duck with Braised Cabbage,
    113
Salisbury Steak with Quick Mash, 132
Salmon Niçoise Salad, 69
Shepherd's Pie, 134
Speedy Cauliflower-n-Cheese, 117
Steak Fajitas with Avocado Salsa
    Verde, 133
Taco Frittata, 79
Tiramisu Ice Bombs, 140
Toasted Nut Butter, 169
Turkey Nuggets with Kale Slaw &
    Italian Dressing, 84
Turkey Souvlaki with Supergreens
    Salad, 115
Vanilla-Keto Ice Cream, 141
Zucchini Lasagna, 81
Italian Sausage Frittata, 32

J
Jalapeño & Cheese Muffins, 25

K
Ketchup, 161
Keto Cheese Sauce Three Ways, 12
Keto Kung Pao Chicken, 114
Keto "Peanut" Butter Cups, 156–157
Keto Tortillas Three Ways, 11
Key Lime Pie in a Jar, 145

L
Lamb Vindaloo, 135

M
Marinara Sauce, 166
Masala Cauli-Rice with Grilled Halloumi,
    96
Mayonnaise, 163
Mexican Chicken Bowls, 85
Mexican Pulled Pork, 120
Moussaka, 136

N
Nightshade-free recipes
    Almond Bliss Bars, 143
    Avocado-Egg Stuffed Bacon Cups, 47
    Basil Pesto, 167
    Bone Broth, 160
    Boston Cream Pie, 150–151
    Breakfast Egg Muffins Two Ways, 24
    Breakfast Sausage Guac Stacks, 34
    Broccoli & Mushroom Alfredo
        Casserole, 94
    Brownie Almond Cheesecake Bars,
        152
    Carrot Cake Oatmeal, 39
    Chewy Pumpkin and Chocolate Chip
        Cookies, 148
    Chicken Piccata, 110
    Chocolate and Raspberry Truffles,
        142
    Chocolate Chip Pancakes, 42
    Clam Chowder, 63
    Cookie Dough Mousse, 147

Creamy Dark Hot Chocolate, 154
Creamy "Potato" Soup, 65
Crispy Chicken with Olives and
    Lemon, 109
Czech Butter Cake, 144
Dijon Mustard, 162
Fat-Fueled Smoothie Two Ways, 43
Flavored Butter Twelve Ways, 14–15
Fluffy Cocoa & Berry Omelet, 41
Greek Meatball Soup, 60
Greek Zucchini and Feta Fritters, 80
Ham and Cheese Fat Bombs, 46
Ham & Cheese Bread Rolls, 86
Homemade Dark Chocolate Three
    Ways, 16–17
Induction Carbonara, 119
Keto Cheese Sauce Three Ways, 12
Keto "Peanut" Butter Cups, 156–157
Keto Tortillas Three Ways, 11
Key Lime Pie in a Jar, 145
Mayonnaise, 163
"No-Tella" Granola, 40
Pork Carnitas (Mexican Pulled Pork),
    120
Pork Pot Roast with Vegetables, 123
Raspberry Electrolyte Limeade, 155
Roast Duck with Braised Cabbage,
    113
Shepherd's Pie, 134
Skillet Berry Crumble, 146
Snickerdoodle Crème Brûlée, 153
Speedy Cauliflower-n-Cheese, 117
Spiced Berry Chia Jam, 170
Spiced Coconut Granola Bars, 89
Stuffed Avocados Two Ways, 73
Sweet Cinnamon Rolls, 38
Tiramisu Ice Bombs, 140
Toasted Nut Butter, 169
Turkey Souvlaki with Supergreens
    Salad, 115
Vanilla-Keto Ice Cream, 141
Vanilla Panna Cotta with Strawberry
    Coulis, 149
Zucchini Lasagna, 81
"No-Tella" Granola, 40
Nut-free recipes
    Abundance Breakfast Bowls, 27
    Avocado-Egg Stuffed Bacon Cups, 47
    Bacon-Wrapped Beef Patties with
        "Chimiole," 82
    Bacon-Wrapped Chorizo Meatloaf
        with Caramelized Cauliflower,
        128
    Baked Jalapeño Popper Dip, 51
    Basil Pesto, 167
    Beef Bourguignon, 131
    Beef Short Ribs with Coleslaw, 130
    Bone Broth, 160
    Breakfast Egg Muffins Two Ways, 24
    Breakfast Pizza Waffles, 28
    Breakfast Sausage Guac Stacks, 34
    Broccoli & Mushroom Alfredo
        Casserole, 94
    Butter Chicken, 106
    Cajun Andouille Gumbo, 101
    Carne Asada Salad, 71
    Cheese-Stuffed Greek Bifteki, 137
    Cheeseburger Soup, 59
    Chewy Pumpkin and Chocolate Chip
        Cookies, 148

Chicken Caesar Salad with Poached Egg, 72
Chicken Piccata, 110
Chimichurri, 171
Chocolate and Raspberry Truffles, 142
Chocolate Chip Pancakes, 42
Chorizo & Kale Hash, 36
Clam Chowder, 63
Coq au Vin, 105
Creamy Dark Hot Chocolate, 154
Creamy "Potato" Soup, 65
Crispy Chicken with Olives and Lemon, 109
Crispy Ranch Chicken Wings, 53
Dijon Mustard, 162
Easy Italian Breakfast Bake, 37
Eggplant Parma Ham Rolls, 78
Eggs Florentine in Portobello Mushrooms, 22–23
Fat-Fueled Smoothie Two Ways, 43
Flavored Butter Twelve Ways, 14–15
Fluffy Cocoa & Berry Omelet, 41
Greek Breakfast Hash, 35
Greek Briam, 93
Greek Meatball Soup, 60
Greek Zucchini and Feta Fritters, 80
Green Shakshuka, 31
Ham and Cheese Fat Bombs, 46
Harissa Fish Tray Bake, 100
Healthy Deconstructed Hamburgers, 127
Healthy Fish Sticks with Tartar Sauce, 97
Homemade Dark Chocolate Three Ways, 16–17
Hungarian Goulash, 66
Induction Carbonara, 119
Italian Sausage Frittata, 32
Ketchup, 161
Keto Cheese Sauce Three Ways, 12
Key Lime Pie in a Jar, 145
Lamb Vindaloo, 135
Marinara Sauce, 166
Masala Cauli-Rice with Grilled Halloumi, 96
Mayonnaise, 163
Mexican Chicken Bowls, 85
Moussaka, 136
Pork Pot Roast with Vegetables, 123
Ranch Salad in a Jar, 70
Raspberry Electrolyte Limeade, 155
Ratatouille Soup, 64
Roast Duck with Braised Cabbage, 113
Salisbury Steak with Quick Mash, 132
Salmon Niçoise Salad, 69
Shepherd's Pie, 134
Slovak Sauerkraut Soup, 56
Snickerdoodle Crème Brûlée, 153
Southern Duck Deviled Eggs, 48
Spanish Eggs, 21
Speedy Cauliflower-n-Cheese, 117
Speedy Keto Crackers, 50
Spiced Berry Chia Jam, 170
Spicy Chocolate BBQ Sauce, 164
Steak Fajitas with Avocado Salsa Verde, 133
Stuffed Avocados Two Ways, 73
Sushi: Spicy Tuna Rolls, 99

Sweet & Sour BBQ Sauce, 165
Taco Frittata, 79
Thai Curry Chicken Tray Bake, 102
Tiramisu Ice Bombs, 140
Turkey Nuggets with Kale Slaw & Italian Dressing, 84
Turkey Souvlaki with Supergreens Salad, 115
Vanilla-Keto Ice Cream, 141
Vanilla Panna Cotta with Strawberry Coulis, 149
Zucchini Lasagna, 81

P
Peri Peri Roasted Nuts, 49
Pizza Two Ways, 124–125
Pork Carnitas (Mexican Pulled Pork), 120
Pork Pot Roast with Vegetables, 123
Pork Schnitzel with Zesty Slaw, 116
Portobello mushrooms
    Eggs Florentine in Portobello Mushrooms, 22–23

R
Ranch Salad in a Jar, 70
Raspberry Electrolyte Limeade, 155
Ratatouille Soup, 64
Red Pesto, 168
Roast Duck with Braised Cabbage, 113

S
Salisbury Steak with Quick Mash, 132
Salmon Niçoise Salad, 69
Shepherd's Pie, 134
Skillet Berry Crumble, 146
Slovak Sauerkraut Soup, 56
Snickerdoodle Crème Brûlée, 153
Sourdough Keto Buns, 10
Southern Duck Deviled Eggs, 48
Spanish Eggs, 21
Speedy Cauliflower-n-Cheese, 117
Speedy Keto Crackers, 50
Spiced Berry Chia Jam, 170
Spiced Coconut Granola Bars, 89
Spicy Chocolate BBQ Sauce, 164
Steak Fajitas with Avocado Salsa Verde, 133
Stuffed Avocados Two Ways, 73
Sushi: Spicy Tuna Rolls, 99
Sweet Cinnamon Rolls, 38
Sweet & Sour BBQ Sauce, 165

T
Taco Frittata, 79
Thai Curry Chicken Tray Bake, 102
Tiramisu Ice Bombs, 140
Turkey Nuggets with Kale Slaw & Italian Dressing, 84
Turkey Souvlaki with Supergreens Salad, 115

V
Vanilla-Keto Ice Cream, 141
Vanilla Panna Cotta with Strawberry Coulis, 149
Vegetable Rose Pie, 77
Vegetarian recipes
    Almond Bliss Bars, 143
    Basil Pesto, 167
    Boston Cream Pie, 150–151

Breakfast Egg Muffins Two Ways, 24
Breakfast Sausage Guac Stacks, 34
Broccoli & Mushroom Alfredo Casserole, 94
Brownie Almond Cheesecake Bars, 152
Carrot Cake Oatmeal, 39
Chewy Pumpkin and Chocolate Chip Cookies, 148
Chimichurri, 171
Chocolate and Raspberry Truffles, 142
Chocolate Chip Pancakes, 42
Cookie Dough Mousse, 147
Creamy Dark Hot Chocolate, 154
Creamy "Potato" Soup, 65
Czech Butter Cake, 144
Dijon Mustard, 162
Fat-Fueled Smoothie Two Ways, 43
Flavored Butter Twelve Ways, 14–15
Fluffy Cocoa & Berry Omelet, 41
Greek Breakfast Hash, 35
Greek Briam, 93
Greek Zucchini and Feta Fritters, 80
Green Shakshuka, 31
Homemade Dark Chocolate Three Ways, 16–17
Jalapeño & Cheese Muffins, 25
Ketchup, 161
Keto Cheese Sauce Three Ways, 12
Keto "Peanut" Butter Cups, 156–157
Key Lime Pie in a Jar, 145
Marinara Sauce, 166
Masala Cauli-Rice with Grilled Halloumi, 96
Mayonnaise, 163
"No-Tella" Granola, 40
Peri Peri Roasted Nuts, 49
Raspberry Electrolyte Limeade, 155
Ratatouille Soup, 64
Red Pesto, 168
Skillet Berry Crumble, 146
Snickerdoodle Crème Brûlée, 153
Sourdough Keto Buns, 10
Southern Duck Deviled Eggs, 48
Spanish Eggs, 21
Speedy Keto Crackers, 50
Spiced Berry Chia Jam, 170
Spiced Coconut Granola Bars, 89
Spicy Chocolate BBQ Sauce, 164
Stuffed Avocados Two Ways, 73
Sweet Cinnamon Rolls, 38
Sweet & Sour BBQ Sauce, 165
Tiramisu Ice Bombs, 140
Toasted Nut Butter, 169
Vanilla-Keto Ice Cream, 141
Vegetable Rose Pie, 77

Z
Zucchini Lasagna, 81